CULTURE JOCK

One Foot In The World,
One Foot In The Church

KENNY NOBLE CORTES

Copyright © 2024 Kenny Noble Cortes.

All rights reserved. No part of this book may be reproduced, stored, or transmitted by any means—whether auditory, graphic, mechanical, or electronic—without written permission of both publisher and author, except in the case of brief excerpts used in critical articles and reviews. Unauthorized reproduction of any part of this work is illegal and is punishable by law.

Unless otherwise indicated, all Scripture quotations are taken from the Holy Bible, New Living Translation, copyright © 1996, 2004, 2015 by Tyndale House Foundation. Used by permission of Tyndale House Publishers, Carol Stream, Illinois 60188. All rights reserved.

DISCLAIMER: Culture Jock depicts actual events in the life of the author as truthfully as recollection permits and/or can be verified by research. Occasionally, dialogue consistent with the character or nature of the person speaking has been supplemented. All persons within are actual individuals; there are no composite characters. The names of some individuals have been changed to respect their privacy.

ISBN: 979-8-89419-325-0 (sc)
ISBN: 979-8-89419-326-7 (hc)
ISBN: 979-8-89419-327-4 (e)

Because of the dynamic nature of the Internet, any web addresses or links contained in this book may have changed since publication and may no longer be valid. The views expressed in this work are solely those of the author and do not necessarily reflect the views of the publisher, and the publisher hereby disclaims any responsibility for them.

One Galleria Blvd., Suite 1900, Metairie, LA 70001
(504) 702-6708

"You can't worship two gods at once.
Loving one god, you'll end up hating the other.
Adoration of one feeds contempt for the other.
You can't worship God and Money both."
—Matthew 6:24 MSG

CONTENTS

Dedication vii
Foreword ix
Preface xiii
Introduction xvii

Chapter 1   Space City or Bust 1
Chapter 2   About Face 7
Chapter 3   Oh, Kay! 20
Chapter 4   Persona non Persona: Who am I? 39
Chapter 5   The Self I Served 47
Chapter 6   Brace yourself!!! 59
Chapter 7   Listeners: Chummy or Chumpy? 70
Chapter 8   Busted flat in Chicago? 84
Chapter 9   L.A. Part One—Cowabunga!! 102
Chapter 10 Fasten Your Seatbelts 113
Chapter 11 L.A. Part Two—Disaster 127
Chapter 12 When Push Comes To Shove 136
Chapter 13 Miracle of Miracles 159
Chapter 14 Mile High Dreams 172
Chapter 15 Reckoning and Redemption 183
Chapter 16 Saving the Best for Last 188

Acknowledgements 203
Airchecks and Interviews 209
Timeline 211
Reviews 213

DEDICATION

Culture Jock is dedicated to my wife Kay. It was Kay who introduced me to Jesus many years ago. It was Kay who stuck with me through thin and thinner, and it is Kay who is now quadriplegic following her cardiac arrest and cessation of breathing for more than ten minutes, resulting in severe anoxia. I love you so much, Babe. Anything good in me began with you.

FOREWORD

by Richie Furay

Culture Jock is the brutally honest story of one guy, Kenny Noble Cortes' journey in a fallen world as he navigates the slippery slope of life with "One Foot in the World, One Foot in the Church" all, while holding on to the promise Jesus gave to Believers in John 14:1-3.

> *1 "Let not your heart be troubled; you believe in God, believe also in Me.*
>
> *2 "In My Father's house are many mansions; if it were not so, I would have told you. I go to prepare a place for you.*
>
> *3 "And if I go and prepare a place for you, I will come again and receive you to Myself; that where I am, there you may be also.*

There is a misconception that the Christian life on this earth is "blue skies, green lights and tops down weather" but Kenny's story tells the truth – Christians face every obstacle in life that every other person faces, we laugh, we cry, we have mountain top experiences, and we fall flat on our face from stupidity and wrong choices just like everyone else. Regardless, the "Key" to our future is Jesus who loves us unconditionally and though He will chasten those whom He loves – He is a merciful and forgiving Savior.

I don't know Kenny personally although it seems our lives should have crossed at some time or another, but I know his back-story all too well, personally! I met him in Chapter 16 of his book while reading his posts on social media. It was heart wrenching to say the least. I knew nothing of his background until I read *Culture Jock*, only knowing what I read on social media; it touched me deeply as he spoke of his wife Kay, his love for her and his devotion to her as he was now her caregiver because of complications from an illness. If ever agape love was demonstrated in fallen man, this is an example to behold.

The important take away and why I hope you'll read his book is because it is an honest story of a Believer, saved by grace making his way through the jungle of life's ups and down's, holding on for dear life – because sometimes we get off the path, into the weeds and wonder – can we ever be forgiven by our loved ones or by the One we call Lord and Savior? Only to be reminded:

> *5 Trust in the LORD with all your heart, and lean not on your own understanding;*
>
> *6 In all your ways acknowledge Him, and He shall direct your paths.*
>
> Proverbs 3:5,6

And...

> *If we confess our sins, He is faithful and just to forgive us our sins and to cleanse us from all unrighteousness.* 1 John 1:8

Richie Furay is an American music luminary, a Colorado Music Hall of Fame and Rock & Roll Hall of Fame inductee. He is celebrated for pioneering Country-Rock as founding member of the legendary and quintessential groups Buffalo Springfield, Poco, and the Souther-Hillman-Furay band.

Courtesy www.richiefuray.com/

PREFACE

Culture Jock is a name I've carried with me for years so that one day, far off into the future, I would write my book. My goodness, how time flies like an arrow (and fruit flies like a banana) ☺ I never dreamed I would ever be retired and on Social Security along with my wife, Kay.

'Culture Jock' is a play on the term, *culture shock*, two words that describe what may happen when someone visits another country or in the not-too-distant future, another planet! (Let *that* roll around in your head.) And the local culture is much different than they are accustomed to – precisely my family's 43-year journey from conservative upbringing in the church to the struggle of maintaining our family values through the complex and pitfall-laden world of broadcasting.

The actual catalyst to write the book, however, came from Pruitt Health Hospice, the dear people caring for Kay as she lay quiet and quadriplegic. Their chaplain, Jim Crews, called to stop by, to pray, and to bring some encouragement and sandwiches… or "sammiches" as he refered to them. In the last year that I have been Kay's caregiver, Jim has stopped by every couple of weeks, and he never fails to bring a "sammich."

On one visit, he said he had written a book – not for publishing, but for his family as a legacy of sorts. He, like me, is a child of the 60s and has had quite an interesting life. So, thank you Jim for that encouragement and for kindling a spark in my heart to write this book. It's an honest book because I reveal more of my sinful nature than I would in person. (Unless I were confessing those sins to another) So please go easy on me and hopefully you will learn from my mistakes. *Culture Jock* will surely give you many of those opportunities.

Finally, with respect to the timeline, there are several instances where I write outside of the normal chronology to continue the topic. My stories about flying and surfing are two examples. Sometimes there were years between flying lessons and my 'adventures' but I wanted to maintain the flying narrative for continuity's sake. The same is mostly true about my surfing experiences. I made an exception in this instance because of a natural break in the narrative.

I believe it is important to the reader to bring closure to stories that are best told from start to finish, like our son Sam's near drowning, and the conclusion of the consequences of his survival as it related to me some 12 years later; this was crucial to the story.

There are two more stories that have dramatic conclusions 14 years later and 8 years after the characters are introduced. In each case, I return to the timeline, but it may seem to some that the chronology is out of sequence… and in fact, it is, to bring closure to these two far-reaching stories. I tried to present my chronology 'deviations' as flashbacks or flash forwards in a movie.

The consequences of Pastor Jimmy's actions and those of Program Director Jeremy Smith directly impact the chronology precisely because there are long periods between their introduction to the narrative and to their respective denouement years later. In each case, I pick up the timeline where it was left off when we 'time-jumped' a decade or more into the future. But to some, it may be a little confusing to return to the point where I left the timeline and began filling in the events that occurred during the decade or so that were also essential but not germane to the narrative at hand.

I've included a timeline chart that doesn't jump around, per se, but follows major events as they occurred in the order they did so. It's at the back of the book.

I have learned a great deal about myself while writing these personal accounts. Most of it is unflattering and I'm not proud of my selfish actions or by the practice of frequently putting my needs first. Completing this book has been eye-opening to say the least. It is not fun or comfortable to be confronted by images that reflect who we really are. Our spiritual mirrors do not lie.

I sincerely hope you are blessed through lessons learned in these stories, alas, most of us learn the hard way. Thank you for reading Culture Jock (One Foot in The World, One Foot in The Church). May God bless you through your own journey.

INTRODUCTION

I was born in Tampa, Florida—a post war baby boomer, the son of a WWII vet. After the war, my dad, Clymer M. Noble, Jr. married his sweetheart, Mary Alice Cortes. I am a first generation American on my mom's side. At twelve years old, along with her mother and three siblings, she immigrated to the U.S. through Ellis Island, New York from Bogota, Colombia. My parents said their vows in December 1945 and were married for forty-two years. Dad passed away in 1988; Mom in 1999.

By age three, we had moved to Richmond, California so dad could go to college on the V.A. He graduated with a degree in petroleum engineering in 1954 and worked for Shell Chemical's Martinez, California plant for most of his college years. He was transferred following graduation to Shell's sprawling refinery in Deer Park, Texas, near Houston, where he remained until 1984. Following two years at Al Jubail, Saudi Arabia, he finally retired from Shell in 1986. He and mom settled in Lutz, Florida. An upscale community near Tampa.

+++

I was five years old and we were still living in Richmond on Downer Ave. (Seriously, 'Downer') It was the 50s, life was good, home was a happy place, and ignorance of the future was bliss.

One Saturday, dad was using an old-fashioned push mower – no gas, and no power other than sheer muscles. Kids today don't understand what taking forever to mow the lawn really means. He did this every Saturday in the summer. One day, I asked him, "Dad, what makes grass grow?"

He thought for a moment and then gave me an answer. Dad, in his wisdom, said, "God… God makes grass grow." He didn't elaborate and the fact that he gave me a straight answer was all I needed to hear at my tender age.

But what he did was monumental in that for the first time in my short life, I knew there was something 'out there' that was greater than my dad, who up until now, was the most powerful being in my life. At a very young age, I knew there were greater forces in the world than what I could see. Knowing our place in the universe produces humility. I'm not sure how much humility was produced at age five, but I now know humility is the first step toward submission to God's will which, unlike our own will, builds character and reinforces integrity. It is a fundamental action that leads us toward denial of self – the crown of Christianity and the heart of any believer.

Unknowingly, while simply mowing the lawn, dad planted the seeds of hope within me. The hope of someday learning more about who this 'God' is.

We moved from the San Francisco Bay Area's year-round cool, cloudy weather to a community where the heat and humidity tag-teamed Houstonians like sumo wrestlers in a sauna. Mom never forgave Dad. "We're moving where????? *Ay, Dios mio*! (Oh my God!) Help us!"

Growing up in Houston with my two brothers and a sister in the late 50s and 60s was an exciting experience. Mom and Dad were kind of a reverse Lucy and Ricky. Anytime mom got angry (or emotional) she would rattle off a dozen Spanish words that none of us knew the meaning of. Probably a good thing.

It was a good time to be a kid. We had so much freedom. We lived in the Pasadena-South Houston area so dad's commute to Deer Park wasn't too bad—about a half hour at most. In the summer months, holidays, and Saturdays, we would take off on our bikes and be gone almost all day.

Kids today are growing up in a world where they have no idea what it means to not worry about predators, sexual or otherwise. Back then, so-called "gangs" were more like the Jets and the Sharks in 'West Side Story'. They didn't resemble anything close to the Crips and Bloods or MS-13 in East L.A. and other urban areas.

Aside from the usual stuff kids got into… like smoking cigs in school or tossing spitballs at the students in front, *we* were rowing down Brays Bayou in a makeshift boat made from corrugated aluminum that we 'borrowed' from a construction site. Barely two inches of *The Shark* was visible above the water line, I would shout, "Keep still guys! There are alligator gars, snapping turtles and water moccasins all over the place! DON'T ROCK THE BOAT!!!" Eeesh. Could Captain Bligh have sounded more obnoxious?

Speaking of boats, one of my brother Larry's passions is boats. He LOVES boats and has owned several over his lifetime including a few make-shift boats. To say my younger brother Larry is creative would be an understatement. He was born with a crayon in one hand and a lump of clay in the other. Today my brother is a world-renowned artist/sculptor with dozens of statues around the country and in some parts of the world. Google Lawrence Noble sometime. But I digress.

When he was about nine years old, he had a makeshift boat – *The Sea Tiger*, which was square. Remember I said he had a knack for creativity, not engineering. You don't see many square boats out there unless they're a barge or a houseboat or something that doesn't move very quickly. Even a bathtub would have been faster.

Nevertheless, *The Sea Tiger* was about four or five feet from side to side… to side. It was made from 1x12 planks and had a 'seat' at the front and back… or maybe on each side, hard to say with a square boat, but you get the idea. In the middle of the boat, was a single plank that at first resembled one of the seats, but it had a hole in the middle of it for a mast and sail. Yes, you read that right, a square sailboat! Not exactly the most seaworthy of boats. It had a rudder of sorts and was about as stable as a house of cards; ready to disassemble itself at the first breath of stormy weather. But Larry wasn't going to take it out in stormy weather… or was he?

Once the boat was completely built and painted a rich forest green, he made a sail from a sheet (I think he just took one from the laundry) and now all he needed was a place to try it out. 'Luckily', mother nature provided a flood that overflowed Brays Bayou, just a hundred yards or so away from our house which was located at the high end of a slope that banked down to the swollen stream. The flood was epic and produced a bayou about the size of the Mississippi River! Well, it was big and wide and filled with a treacherous current. No worries. Larry said this was perfect. Ah, the wisdom of a nine-year-old. Although I was two years older,

I didn't try to stop him, why would I? I was curious to see how this would play out.

We carried the boat to the edge of the water which was now creeping up our street having overflowed the banks of the bayou. Larry had his Captain's hat on and asked me to give him a big shove. But first, we had to break a bottle of champagne to bless the boat. We didn't have champagne, so we used a bottle of Delaware Punch. The bottle didn't break, which normally meant the ship was unlucky, but no matter. Before you know it. There he was, Master and Commander of *The Sea Tiger*– a square boat that was slowly and precariously drifting toward the current. The neighborhood kids cheered him on!

At that moment, dad stepped out of the house to see what all the fuss was about, saw his son drifting away toward certain calamity and raced into the water to fetch *The Sea Tiger*. Which he did… but barely before the current became swift indeed! The neighborhood kids who had all gathered for the big launching helped dad rescue Captain Horatio Larry Hornblower and *The Sea Tiger*.

Sadly, once *The Sea Tiger* was safe on dry pavement, dad methodically kicked, thrashed, mashed, trampled, and dismantled the boat that Larry had so meticulously put together with nails, old planks, and masking tape. He snapped the mast in two, ripped the sail into shreds and then piled *The Sea Tiger* into so much flotsam to be tossed into the trash never to see the light of day again. King Josiah, who rid the temple of Baals, Ashtaroth's and false gods, would have been proud!

> *Under his (Josiah's) direction the altars of the Baals were torn down; he cut to pieces the incense altars that were above them and smashed the Asherah poles and the idols. These he broke to pieces and scattered over the graves of those who had sacrificed to them.* 2 Chronicles 34:4,5

He threatened Larry with the same fate if he EVER DID THAT AGAIN! Which he didn't.

Yeppers, growing up in Houston was an adventure! Oh, I almost forgot to mention the occasional hopping of trains at the local train yard. And uh, we didn't check with our parents first.

+++

I sailed through Henderson Elementary, Queen of Peace Catholic School, ninth grade at Mt. Carmel High School and transferred to Stephen F. Austin public High School in 1963 when mom and dad could no longer afford parochial school tuition. I'll never forget, Queen of Peace had the legendary Sister Mary Godzilla (name changed to protect the innocent) who single-handedly took the star quarterback of our eighth-grade team and with one hand thrust him against the wall threatening him with a metal ruler—which she wielded like a Samurai sword and used to intimidate

Ronnie B with a warning to NEVER, EVER heckle her again. Oh yeah, that was worth the price of admission!

+++

The best and worst experience for my family happened in November 1963. President John F. Kennedy's entourage came through Houston on November 21. My mom was a huge fan of President Kennedy and took us all to the Gulf Freeway (only a half mile from the house) to see the President and First Lady. We were in the front row when the motorcade passed by. He was the only President I have ever seen in person. Sadly, JFK was fatally shot the next day in Dallas.

When we heard the news, everyone, and I mean everyone, was crying, sobbing or distraught. The assassination of JFK seemed to usher in a series of high-profile deaths including the Reverend Martin Luther King, Jr., Bobby Kennedy, Jim Morrison, Janis Joplin, Jimi Hendrix, and many others throughout the 60s and 70s. Their contributions to civil rights, music, politics, college age experimentation with dangerous drugs, and the anti-Vietnam War movement would ultimately define the 'Me Generation.'

+++

This new 'revolution', as described by John Lennon and many other artists and film celebrities, helped usher in moral relativism—a seductive philosophy that replaces Godly principles in tiny, but effective steps. Basically, what's right for you isn't necessarily right for me. By the mid-80s, divorce rates had skyrocketed. Stigma over sexual orientation, personal ethics, and respect for Christian principles, as well as Christians themselves, was on the decline.

Broadcasters, who at first were banned from using the words 'hell' or 'damn' in TV and radio programs, were soon using language that proved less and less shocking as the years flew by. Western culture was morphing into its own evil doppelganger before our very eyes and ears.

In a profession that cultivated a lifestyle for singles, raising a family in such an atmosphere was a huge challenge. Against all odds and frequent failures to maintain Christian standards of morality, my wife Kay, our two daughters and two sons prevailed. But I made many mistakes along the way and at times my judgment of what was said *on* the air and what I did *off* the air must have seemed ridiculously absent as I straddled life with one foot in the world and one foot in the church—one of the most overused 'dance' routines known to mankind, and just like everyone else who's tried it, I looked comfortably foolish.

+++

CHAPTER 1

SPACE CITY OR BUST

"You'll never know what you can do until you try."
– Bob Stevens

I leaned forward in my rusty '69 Nova to turn up a song on the radio. It was 'Just My Imagination' on KULF 710 AM in Houston. My favorite deejay Hal McLain was doing what he did best– making me (and all the other fans) feel right at home. (Later I would model my style after McLain. I loved the way he was just himself on the radio.)

As my thoughts meandered, I keyed in on a commercial that was all about getting into the radio business. This sounded interesting. I wasn't happy with my job at Southwest Construction Materials where I drove an eighteen-foot bobtail truck delivering construction materials at various sites around Houston. I knew I could do better than that.

My mind began wandering back to our trek in a 1950 Ford across the desert when we moved from Richmond, California to Houston, Texas.

+++

I was seven years old. It was 1954 and cars didn't come equipped with air conditioning. So, Dad got us a metal tube-thing about 6 inches in diameter... maybe 16 inches long, that was connected to a box containing dry ice. It was slung across the top of the passenger side window and looked more like a homemade mortar launcher than some kind of air conditioner. And... it didn't work! So, it looked like we were going to flop-sweat all the way to Houston.

And we did.

Thankfully, we arrived intact without too much dehydration. Dad bought us a house with a V.A. loan for $7000. It came with an attic fan that sucked hot, steamy air inside and whooshed it around. Kinda worked, but it droned like there was a lawn mower on the roof.

Many people still thought of Houston as the 'Wild West' where folks rode horses and bellied up to saloons for bottomless shots of whiskey. Not exactly. For example, NASA had its eye on the 'Bayou City' as a new center for the burgeoning space agency. Here's why: Houston is a major energy and tech center, has excellent freeways, low cost of living, an international airport and the Port of Houston which is easily accessible from the Gulf of Mexico.

As soon as Houston was selected as the city to build their headquarters, 'Space City' signs began popping up like dandelions in the early spring. They were attached to every business imaginable. 'Space City Icehouse' ("Serving beer as cold as Mars"), 'Space City Guns' ("Ride shotgun with us!"), 'Space City Boots' ("Tired of stepping into hot, steamin' cow patties? Try easy-to-clean Space City boots") 'Space City Baubles, Bangles and Buckles'… this *was* Texas after all.

There was a lot of new construction and NASA was throwing up temporary office buildings all around the Houston metro including a mere half mile from our home in the southeast part of town. Space was certainly invading our town, including the "space" people. One morning on our way to school, mom almost ran over astronauts Gordon Cooper, Gus Grissom and Alan Shepard who were crossing the street and had to quickly step back as we went by all bug-eyed and in awe. Funny, because they were bug-eyed as well. One of them made a gesture with his hand toward our car but I was too young to know what that meant.

+++

Recollections of my first radio go back to 1955, South Houston. When I was eight years old, Dad gave me a crystal radio set. It came with cool headphones and was alligator-clipped to the chain link fence just outside my window. On game nights, I fell asleep listening to Houston Buffs baseball games. Mom would come in later and tenderly remove the headphones while I often pretended to be asleep so I could soak in her sweetness.

As I grew older my love for radios also grew. I carefully put together a Knight Kit, 50-watt transmitter and called Dad out to the garage to watch me plug it in. As soon as the juice hit the radio, it went 'ka-BLOO-ee' with black smoke rising from it like a miniature mushroom cloud. I was devastated. "What. Just. Happened???? Dad helped me re-solder every connection and when we plugged it in again a week later, it worked!

My Novice Class amateur radio call letters were WN5IFY and thanks to the Boy Scouts, I knew morse code backwards and forwards...but mostly forwards, LOL. This allowed me to communicate with other ham operators in twenty-three states as well as my best childhood friend, Nicky Wallingford. We practiced morse code for the Boy Scouts on our local homemade telegraphs connected by copper wire to our homes and strung across Mrs. Gaskal's ½ acre yard. We didn't ask permission of course. - . - - - - . -

Novice Class ham radio operators are restricted to CW or Continuous Wave, meaning they turn the 'wave' or the high-pitched tone on and off with a telegraph key in a series of dots and dashes to spell out words. It was very similar to long distance communication in the late 1800s. In fact, President Abraham Lincoln contacted his generals every morning for the latest battlefield reports during the Civil War via the White House telegraph office. Basically, the telegraph was high-tech communication – de facto texting for the 19th Century.

I was also inspired by my brother Larry who loved CB radios. We had Heath Kits that Dad helped us build. Our walkie-talkies were blazingly powerful, broadcasting a tenth of a watt! Whoa! Imagine that!!! A tenth of a watt!!! We could talk to each other as far as... what... 50 feet away? We could have accomplished the same thing with a Dixie Cup and string... or yelling, but what's the fun in that?

Sadly, my early radio career careened to a screeching halt. Novice ham radio licenses were only good for one year and I would have had to learn a bunch of electrical stuff to get a general class license but, having just turned sixteen, was more interested in the 'fumes— car-fumes and per-fumes'

+++

Back to the future (1972), I pulled into the Southwest Construction Materials parking lot just as a commercial promoting CSB –the Columbia School of Broadcasting (not affiliated with CBS) began. CEO Bob Stevens' gravelly voice announced, *"You'll never know what you can do until you try."* As the commercial faded into endless repetitions of CSB's phone number, I made a mental note to give him a call. Stevens was the owner/manager of the Houston office of Columbia School of Broadcasting. I began to visualize myself as a deejay. "Nah, that couldn't be me. No way could I ever talk that much."

Little did I know I could. Or, that the very microphone I would use to broadcast my voice to millions would also become a gateway to immoral choices, with a few that chased and followed me, more persistently than Wile E. Coyote chased the Road Runner, my entire forty-three-year radio career.

CHAPTER 2

ABOUT FACE

"The pants didn't need me in them to stand up straight."

Before I got to my radio career, I took a slight detour towards the armed services. Which was somewhat expected since my family had a long, rich history of service to the nation. Dad flew twenty-nine missions over Europe in a B-24 Liberator kicking Hitler's butt. My grandfather served during WWI and my great, great, grandfather tore it up at the Battle of Chickamauga during the Civil War. We are also honored to have a direct line of descent to George Clymer, signer of the Declaration of Independence.

On the other hand, mom claimed she was descended from Hernando Cortes, one of the great pillagers of all time. Cortes was a Spanish Conquistador famously known for leading an expedition that caused the fall of the Aztec Empire. Way to go, Mom.

Despite her 'outlaw' roots, Mom encouraged me to follow in dad's footsteps and join the Reserve Officers Training Corp (R.O.T.C.). As a student at Stephen F. Austin High School, I was much more interested in listening to the records getting a lot of airplays at the time –Leslie Gore's *It's My Party*, Skeeter Davis's *End of The World* and Kyu Sakamoto's beautiful *Sukiyaki*. I should have listened to my heart back then. Music had almost always lit my passions. But in 1963, my sophomore year, I decided to learn "leadership excellence" and signed up for the R.O.T.C. program.

CULTURE JOCK

Presenting the colors: James Mondragon, Kenneth Noble, Steve Baker, David Davis and Mike McArdle

For the program, I wore a well-starched khaki uniform twice a week. How much starch? Well, the pants didn't need me in them to stand up straight. Once I had stepped into my uniform, I felt like the Robot in the original *Lost in Space* TV series flailing his metallic arms and shouting "Danger, Will Robinson, Danger."

We learned a lot of things in 'RAHT-see' as we were frequently and derisively referred to by students outside the program. For example, trench foot results from living in your boots with your feet soaked to the bone for too many days at a time. The feet get soggy, then infected, then swollen… and after a while, they smell bad (or worse than usual). They not only hurt, but they kinda look like overcooked eggplant.

We also learned how to assemble and disassemble an M-1 rifle and qualify on the range with our M-1s. Guns allowed in school—that's something you won't find in today's schools. Surprisingly, we had an armory stocked with hundreds of M-1s and a few carbines. They were standard issue in WWII and the Korean War. Kinda scary, because if someone back then had wanted to bring ammo to school, there was nothing to keep them from going 'ballistic'. It was a different time and culture. Common sense and respect for others were the glue of American society. Accountability, right and wrong, as well as responsibility for our actions, were taught at home. We looked out for each other.

A large and fun part of ROTC training was experienced during infrequent weekend bivouacs in the Big Thicket of East Texas—an area choked with trees, loose cattle, deer, rattlesnakes, and wild hogs. We were divided into friendly and aggressor forces then issued our M-1s along with boxes of blank ammunition. On the very first one I attended; we were having a great time until we had… "a situation".

During our 'conflict', one of the aggressor forces caught three of the friendly forces. He pointed his rifle at all three saying, "You're my prisoners."

He then pressed the end of his rifle into one of his captive's backsides, right above the kidney area. I suppose he was about to proudly march his captors away but, before he had time to celebrate his victory, a friendly force guy came up behind the captor and said, "You're *MY* prisoner!"

The first captor freaked out and fired his weapon.

The blank went through the 'prisoner's' cammies, t-shirt, skin and into his stomach lining. Although it had been an accident, the kid was bleeding and needed medical attention. You might be thinking what some of us were thinking that day, "Hey, I thought these were blanks!!" Yes, but, as we learned that day, the only difference between a blank cartridge and a 'live' cartridge is the cap. One is capped with a bullet (projectile), the other is capped with cardboard that at close range can easily penetrate flesh and in some cases could be lethal.

Fact: A blank fired from an M-1 at close range should be treated as if the M-1 is loaded with a 30.06 caliber bullet.

I continued R.O.T.C. for three years. In my senior year, I was encouraged to join one of the services. I chose the Air Force because I wanted to fly. And because dad was in the Air Force Reserve. To accomplish that, I applied to the United States Air Force Academy (USAFA). But soon found it wasn't easy to get in. The appointment process involved contacting your congressman and/or senator and competing with everyone else who was also applying for entry into a service academy, i.e., Air Force, Army, Navy, Coast Guard or Merchant Marine.

I didn't make that first cut but learned about a back door entrance. I could enlist in the USAF as a reservist and attend the USAFA Preparatory School where the odds were greater than 90% an applicant would get an appointment. Much easier that way but of course it would necessitate a year's delay. Most of us—about two hundred— who utilized this backdoor approach didn't mind the wait.

To make things even more interesting, the year was 1965 and the U.S. was smack in the middle of the Vietnam War with the draft very much alive. I had a high draft number. A low draft number meant your chances of getting drafted increased. In any case, I wasn't worried about the draft. I wanted to serve.

The hard part was going to basic training at Lackland AFB, San Antonio, Texas in July. Good golly Miss Molly, "it's so hot and sticky in San Antonio during the summer that your sheets get up when you do!!" (Rim shot) "How hot was it? It was so hot all the snakes were hanging straight down!" ('nuther rim shot)

Following graduation from Air Force basic training, we boarded a flight to Peterson Field, Colorado Springs, Colorado and were then bused to the USAFA Prep School.

The preparatory school is on the same beautiful campus as the Air Force Academy, sitting at about 7,000 feet along the Rampart Range—Foothills to the Rockies. Our mascot was the husky. "We are the huskies, the mighty, mighty huskies. Everywhere we go-oh, people want to know-oh, who we are-are, so we tell them…" yada, yada, yada.

I attended all the classes which included intense training in math, literature, English skills, along with taking the S.A.T. six times! We were allowed to submit the highest score to the AFA for consideration for entrance. I maxed the math and only missed one of the verbal skills questions. I was confident of my chances. Prep School graduation ceremonies were low key for the most part. Mom and dad drove up from Houston, May 10, 1966–on a day that we received ten inches of heavy, wet snow. We all loved it!

The summer of '66 began with the good news that I had received my appointment to the United States Air Force Academy (USAFA). I had only graduated from the USAFA Preparatory School a couple of weeks earlier. Finally, after three years of Army R.O.T.C., six weeks of basic training at Lackland followed by another six weeks of basic training at the USAFA Prep School, I pretty much had the basics down.

I was ready for the United States Air Force Academy.

At the AFA, I was carrying an academic load of twenty-seven hours and spent most of my time studying, which included physical training. It was super hard. The Academy also had a strict honor code. Bust it and you're tossed out. On reflection, I could have used such an honor code when I got into radio. In the military, I didn't have time to get into trouble. That would dramatically change within three years of becoming a deejay, but I'm getting ahead of myself.

One of the coolest things I ever did was to stoop under an open, plexiglass canopy and climb into the back seat of a T-33, 'T-Bird' jet trainer. All cadets were required to take a 30-minute ride on the T-Bird to get the feel of the aircraft and obviously to motivate (or scare the hell out of you) thus weeding out those who were not cut out for pilot training.

They handed me a parachute, a helmet with oxygen mask, and two-way com with the pilot, whom I was sitting immediately behind, and we took off from Pete Field (Today known as Peterson AFB). My pilot took off almost vertically so fast that the water molecules in the air instantly sublimated to snow or ice crystals inside and underneath the clear jet canopy that allowed us an awesome 360-degree view of the sky. We roared to 10,000 feet in a flash – the canopy 'snow' an amazing sight that only lasted for a few seconds. I was stoked! After flying past the Royal Gorge, we turned and headed for home. I asked the pilot if he could do a barrel roll and without answering he initiated the roll, making my day... my year!! This final acrobatic maneuver would be reprised for me in about 15 years by a Korean war vet in a Navy SNJ-2 trainer. (More on that in Chapter 10.)

By all appearances, I was on my way to becoming a pilot in the Air Force. Back then, graduates would be off to pilot school and shuffled out to Southeast Asia for service in the Vietnam War. In late June, I began my new life as a 4th class cadet and member of the Class of '70.

However, by the beginning of my second semester as a 'Doolie', the nickname given to 4th class cadets, I was seriously considering resigning. Things just weren't what I had expected them to be. The grueling workload and strict rules started me thinking that I was really missing out on a lot at home.

Music was tugging at my heart and soul.

I had picked up a guitar and taught myself how to play. My grandmother taught me piano when I was ten years old. Then, I had another year of piano in parochial school, so it didn't take long to 'get it' on my guitar. I loved it!

I learned a lot of folk music by artists like Peter, Paul and Mary, Simon and Garfunkel, and Bob Dylan... stuff like that and I came to the realization that I was more right-brained than left-brained.

My rendezvous with my own conscience was still years away, but the seeds had been planted—musical seeds, yes musical! Christian music on Christian radio networks wouldn't get my attention until 2008. What *did* have my attention were the Beach Boys, Doors, and pretty much anything having to do with the British Invasion.

British Invasion: Songs from pop and rock artists in the UK that were released from late 1963 to the end of the decade.

The messages contained in many secular lyrics can soften our moral responses to inner desires and emotions—even erode our convictions over time. That's because music is spiritual in the sense that it can uplift or encourage. Take for example the Navy Hymn. There is a vast gulf between the use of that powerful song that is often sung at memorial services, and say, 'Mack the Knife', a song that glorifies murder… but in a good way, right?

Good, bad, or ugly, music was calling me and by the time Christmas 1966 rolled around, I had made up my mind. A life in uniform was not for me.

The hazing is what finally did me in. I told my parents that if the Academy had been more like the Prep School, where I was treated with respect, then I might not have resigned, but that was not to be. I was relentlessly belittled and berated by upperclassmen at every opportunity. Their blatant use of name-calling wore me down like an old pencil. I was frequently referred to as 'Squat-jab.'

Yeah, now THERE's an uplifting 'sobriquet'. I hated it.

"HEY SQUAT-JAB. PASS THE MASHED POTATOES AND REMEMBER TO KEEP YOUR BEADY EYES ON YOUR PLATE AND KEEP YOUR MOUTH SHUT! GOT IT???"

"Yes Sir!!!!"

"HEY SQUAT-JAB! I JUST TOLD YOU TO KEEP YOUR MOUTH SHUT!"

It was a typical scene at Mitchell Hall, where all cadets ate their meals. We sat ten to a table. Two 1st class cadets (seniors), two 2nd class cadets (juniors), three 3rd class cadets and three 4th class cadets. The Doolies were required to eat looking down at their plates unless spoken to—a real picnic.

Okay, so they wanted to see if I had any mettle under my 'thin' skin. I honestly believe I could have been a very good pilot (I ended up getting a private pilot's license anyway.) I truly believe great officers can be made from men and women who receive respect, encouragement and have role models and mentors to look up to. Tearing people down is not the way to greatness.

Take for instance my first roommate, Gilbert A. Rovito who, unlike me, stuck it out and graduated in 1970. He was a truly great man who became an American hero. Unfortunately, he was KIA when the helicopter he was piloting was shot down over Cambodia in 1973. Rovito had been promoted to captain only three years after graduation. He was a good friend and I think of him often.

The truth is, I believe it took a degree of courage and a 'pound' of persistence for me to leave. It certainly would have been easier to remain and not deal with all the administrative hoops I had to jump through to get out. But, despite the struggle, in February of 1967 I was finally given a ride to the airport and a ticket home. I was on my way to freedom.

Only problem was, I barely had two years of military service behind me, so I still had four more years to fulfill my military obligation.

It wasn't until a few years later that I questioned whether leaving the Academy was a good thing. I was told by my Prep School 'roomie', John, that I certainly DID the RIGHT thing by leaving honorably because many grads who went into pilot school and then into battle, ended up having to undergo... let's just say... a lot of counseling. He said many of these grads had either 'lost it', were KIA, or wounded in Vietnam. More than a few had to deal with the long-term issue of PTSD.

Okay. So, I made the right decision :) I think... Everybody knows radio people are clean as a whistle with pristine reputations and morals that are as pure as Rocky Mountain snow. Right?

After I got home, I needed to get a plan to finish out my obligation. Well, it just so happened my dad was in the Air Force Reserve. My timing was good because the one enlisted man in my dad's unit, the 1st Censorship Squadron, Detachment 22, was retiring. I applied for his job and got it!! I became their admin specialist and ended up serving out my military obligation at Ellington AFB near Houston with my dad for four great years. How cool is that?

+++

CHAPTER 3

OH, KAY!

"Ok, Noble, let's get this over with."

Throughout life, and as I am reflecting on these stories, one thing I have come to realize is that I'm not prone to learn from others' mistakes. I've got to try things out and make my *own* mistakes. This was especially true when it came to surfing, which I gleefully (and recklessly) resumed after exiting the Academy.

In September 1967, after being home for around six months, a hurricane was churning up the Gulf. This was during the height of the season and Hurricane Beulah was bearing down on Texas somewhere south of Galveston. The storm was so huge it almost took up the entire Gulf of Mexico on the radar. But more importantly, it produced some epic surf.

BIG surf. BIG waves. And in my mind, HAKUNA MATATA waves! That is, I wasn't worried because… hey… I'd never surfed a hurricane before. So, how bad could it get?

Bad.

This was back before leashes were considered important lifesaving equipment for surfers. Although I was twenty and should have had *some* sense, my common sense often reverted to that of a five-year-old when it came to surfing— "Wow, big waves, let's go!"

The waves were about as tall as a single-story house with an A frame roof! They were big but rideable. I knew that riding one was going to be no big deal (yeah, that's my inner 5-year-old talking there) but the first challenge would be getting out to them. I'd have to swim past the beach break which extended far out and where the waves were crashing down, to the open Gulf. The Gulf of Mexico's continental shelf is shallow, so the waves break a LONG way out. Unlike the Pacific where the shelf drops precipitously away from the coast. To get to 'open ocean' waves, I would have to paddle approximately a quarter mile out from shore. I noted there was only one other surfer brave enough (or stupid enough) to attempt surfing that day and that guy didn't paddle out as far as I did. I was on my own.

I paddled furiously to reach the open Gulf. After passing through the 'inside' breakers, I sat on my board 'outside'... like WAY out there and waited for my chance. The jetty was so far away in the distance. I could barely see the shoreline because the waves were so big. I wondered if that was the same kind of image Paul saw when he was shipwrecked and adrift at sea for a day and a night as described in 2 Corinthians 11:25.

> *"Three times I was beaten with rods. Once I was stoned. Three times I was shipwrecked. Once I spent a whole night and a day adrift at sea."*

My chance was finally coming. A set of three waves, each progressively bigger, were heading towards me. I knew if I didn't catch the first wave the second one was going to clean me out. So, I decided to take off. As I caught the first wave, there was a steep drop and I fell off my board. It was launched into 'orbit' while I was plunged toward Davy Jones' Locker. My board was nowhere near me, and I was being furiously tossed about like ice cubes in a blender. Although it felt like I was beneath the water forever I'm sure it was only a matter of seconds before I burst through the surface and snatched a breath of air. That too only lasted a moment before I was beat down under the water again by the second wave. One more breath, followed by a third beating.

The mind is no help in situations like this; flashing images of fishermen catching eleven-foot hammerheads off the jetty. I shook the thought of sharks from my mind and frantically paddled to shore, although a shark frenzy seemed like it might be a walk in the park after battling the fury of the ocean for forty-five minutes. My feet finally touched sand and eventually I made it out of the surf. I shouted Hallelujah… then collapsed… exhausted.

I was a twenty-year-old military-fit man and that ocean had tortured me like a trainer from *Biggest Loser*. Man, was I beat and my desire to catch hurricane waves had been quenched, dried to the bone, and added to the no-fly list. Lesson learned: it's no fun when you might die having fun!

+++

It's 1970—the last year of my obligation to Uncle Sam. My sister, Sandra, a senior at J. Frank Dobie HS in Pasadena, tried introducing me to one of her high school friends, Kay, who was only seventeen. I was six years older than Kay and wasn't all that excited about dating a seventeen-year-old. So, I asked my sister if she really wanted to get me a date, could she hook me up with a twenty- or twenty-one-year-old? We both laughed and I assumed that was that. However, a couple of months later, I was invited to my sister's Christmas party which was on December 21, 1970. Unknown to me, Sandra had also invited Kay.

When we finally did meet, I was immediately attracted to her. And when we sat by the fireplace a little later, listening to Bing Crosby sing 'White Christmas' and she began feeding me roasted marshmallows, well, I was smitten—hook, line and sinker.

In April of 1971, Kay turned eighteen and within a two-week period in early June, she graduated from Dobie HS, I got out of the Air Force, and we got married.

+++

(June 4, 2021, with Kay bedridden, and in the middle of a COVID-19 pandemic, we observed our 50th wedding anniversary. More about that extraordinary celebration in Chapter 16, "Saving the Best for Last.")

+++

Although I decided to leave the Air Force, my passion for flying was still real. So, after I left the Academy, I began my training to pursue my private pilot's license. My first training flight was with my Uncle Pete in 1968. He served as

Crew Chief on a B-47 following the Korean War and knew every nut and bolt on that airplane. He retired from the Air Force and was my instructor as we flew out of Jacksonville Airport, Florida where he worked as the supervisor for Aircraft Service. I had been invited to stay with Uncle Pete during the summer of 1968.

By the end of summer, I was glad to be back home in Houston. I then signed on with a flight training school based at Hobby Airport. A few years later, I took lessons at a flight school in Santa Monica, California where I finally got my solo certificate in December of 1979 just before moving to Seattle and working for KZOK. While there, I took a couple of lessons at Boeing Field.

We were only in Seattle (the first time) a couple of months, so I didn't get to resume flying lessons until after we moved back to Southern California. I continued my lessons at Santa Monica Airport where I finally earned my private pilot's license in 1981.

After passing the written test and going up with an FAA specialist to see if I could actually pilot an airplane, I was awarded my Private Pilot certificate and a year later earned my *Pilot Proficiency Wings, Phase 1*. I could finally, legally, carry passengers.

My first passenger was going to be Kay. I walked around the plane, kicked the tires, examined the pitot tube (aircraft speedometer pronounced 'PEE-toe) to make sure it was clear of any sediment and finished the pre-flight. I then looked at Kay and said "Honey, you have to get a picture of me in front of the plane." It was a Cessna 172. She snapped the shot and, in true Kay form, said "Ok, Noble, let's get this over with." I thought it was hilarious. It ended up being a beautiful day. We flew up the coast to Malibu and back to Santa Monica airport.

Yes, we made it back alive.

+++

Kay and I were only married a short time before we realized somebody had to do the grocery shopping and somebody had to figure out what we were going to eat. That wasn't something we had ever talked about before we were married. But there were some, very clear, lines drawn when it came to food just a few months into our marriage.

One of the things I enjoyed doing when we lived near Clear Lake, southeast of Houston, was fishing. There was a bridge on NASA RD 1 that spanned a creek into Clear Lake – an inlet of Galveston Bay. The bay was saltwater and there are some prime fishing spots for speckled trout near the MSC (Manned Spacecraft Center). There was a rock outcropping from the bridge that went down into the lake. I'd rock dance my way to the water and would usually catch two or three nice sized specks.

We lived less than ten minutes away, and I had let Kay know that I was going fishing. Later, I brought them home in a cooler and said, "Here you go." To which Kay replied, "What do you mean *here you go*?"

I said, "Well, they have to be cleaned. See, you cut the head off like this and then you have to scrape the scales off." (This went over like a barrel at Niagara Falls.)

She said, "I've got this bloody fish here, what am I supposed to do now, Sir Gadabout Gaddis?"

I shrugged my shoulders, "I don't know. Make some rice or something to go with it." This latest attempt at being the 'man of the house' went down like a hawk in a power dive.

We had plain rice and fish for dinner that night, after which I received the following instructions, "You can do this yourself from now on!"

I can't say I was disappointed as it wasn't that good anyway, LOL

+++

If you'll remember in Chapter 1, before I got into the radio business, I drove an eighteen-foot bobtail truck. My co-worker, Freddie, was often my 'co-pilot' and 'partner in crime' on these deliveries. On this day we had a load of construction materials to deliver around Houston. Freddie was asleep in the passenger's seat and I was driving.

Unknown to us, a pair of killers who had tragically murdered a family and child were on the loose in a truck similar to ours. Do you see where this is going? We're just minding our own business. I'm listening to Elton John's *Your Song* on the radio. Freddie is cranking out z's and we're just chillin' to our next delivery.

We were headed out the Southwest Freeway and had just taken the Fondren Road exit when I looked in my sideview mirror and noticed a motorcycle cop riding really fast in our direction on the grass to my immediate left. Before I could say, "Huh?" he slid to a stop right alongside our truck, dismounted his bike and was pointing his Smith & Wesson Model 28 a couple of inches from my forehead and yelling at me to get out of the truck. I was shell-shocked and did what he said.

Meanwhile, another cop had done the same thing to Freddie who was asleep but woke up to a Model 28 in his face as well. He was freaked and kept saying, "Whut?... whu?... whu?...

huh?... whu... huh? It sounded like he wanted to say "Wah, Watusi" but I knew that he wasn't saying that.

The cop who yanked me out of the truck frog-marched me to the back and ordered me to open the door. He asked loudly, "What have you got in there?"

I said, "D-d-d-doors... we have d-d-doors."

When the cops saw the doors and construction materials, they knew they had the wrong guys. They apologized and suggested we stop somewhere and get some coffee. Then as quickly as they appeared, they were gone. Gee, thanks fellas! You only took five years off our lives with that mistaken identity pseudo arrest. It was enough to make you want a drink. I didn't have a drinking problem then, so coffee was fine. Valium would have been better.

However, I can't say when it came to work that I was always clean as a whistle. I had a sneaky way of being sneaky. And that may partly explain why I'm an alcoholic. In the interest of transparency, I now only drink red wine and while I love the taste of beer, I rarely consume it anymore. When I was younger, Cold Duck was my choice of liquids to make me sick. I almost always ended our encounters driving the porcelain bus. Ugh! Seriously, that stuff is bad to the bone. But that didn't stop my partner Freddie and I from consuming the purple poison every Friday while ON THE JOB! This goes back to a time when I had mac and cheese for brains.

But I digress.

On this ill-fated Friday, Freddie and I were assigned to deliver a truck load of prefabricated doors and jams. The eighteen-foot bobtail truck would be full and might be somewhat unwieldy. They tend to be a little top heavy anyway. Translation: take it easy on the turns, bro. Cue Kenny Noble Cortes to the scene, *"Yo no hablo* common sense." (Literal translation: "I do not speak common sense.")

Freddie and I got along famously especially on Friday, and we were up for the trip today because we had a longer haul than usual. We were to deliver our doors and jams to a site in Galveston some fifty miles south of Houston.

By this time, I am a conservative Christian attending a conservative church. Of course, I didn't tell Kay what we did on Fridays. That's because I was a grade A, bona fide, certified, bone-headed hypocrite—AND I was downright stupid. If only I had feared the wrath of God a bit more than the wrath of Kay, maybe I would have walked a straighter line.

On this soon-to-be dysfunctional Friday, Freddie and I proceeded to hit the Gulf Freeway and headed south to Galveston. About five miles north of Galveston we got off on the wrong exit. The frontage road pulled a U-Turn underneath an overpass about a quarter mile away so I figured it wouldn't be too big of a problem. The problem was alcohol, which of course impairs judgement. I was going too fast for the load we were carrying. The recommended speed on the exit ramp was 30mph, I was doing 65mph. Although I could see the turn just ahead, I was still going 60mph. At the last minute, I realized I was going waaaay too fast.

As we rounded the corner to the sharp left turn the truck leaned to its right side. For a brief moment, I'm sure we could have made even the best stunt driver cringe as we popped up on two wheels. Freddie whipped his suntanned right arm back inside the truck. And it's a good thing he did because we hit the pavement hard and slid about fifty feet before coming to rest. We walked to a nearby gas station and called the Texas Highway Patrol. We also ditched the Cold Duck bottle. It was empty of course but amazingly when the troopers showed up, they didn't give sobriety tests, and besides, we were quite sober... appearing.

A bad wreck is a sure-fire buzz killer.

The doors and jams looked like a storm scene right out of tornado alley. We told the troopers that the load shifted. Of course, the only reason it shifted was because I was going too fast but thankfully, we didn't get a ticket and more importantly, nobody was hurt. I quit the job soon after that.

+++

This next trip to Galveston would prove to be less dangerous... physically. But emotionally and morally, a foundation for a house of addiction was being built on sand.

The church that Kay and I attended was a South Houston Bible church. One of the deacons reached out to me. Dan was five or six years older than me, and he invited me to go fishing with him at the pier in Galveston. He was going to pick me up at ten o' clock at night, we would drive to Galveston, fish all night and come home in the morning. This was Kay's church that she had been going to when we met. The year was 1971. I had no idea this would be my first lesson on how to properly be a hypocrite, with on-the-job training from a deacon as a bonus!

When he picked me up, he had a cooler with him. He said he brought some drinks for us. I'm only twenty-four at the time, naive and a new Christian. When we got to our spot on the pier, I opened the cooler and there must have been a whole case of Budweiser in there. I said, "Whoa!"

Dan replied in his real Texan accent, "You can't go fishin' without no beer, you gotta have beer when you're fishin', boy."

The thing is, in that moment, without realizing it, he became a stumbling block for me. I don't blame him for the choices that I made. I didn't have anything against drinking in moderation per se. My parents had their scotch and water every day, but the biggest thing to me was that Dan was a deacon, a leader in the church. And he was telling me it was ok to drink. To some extent, I felt as if I was being given permission to do the thing I had been wanting to do but was conflicted on. I no longer felt as if I was breaking some tradition if I drank. However, where I became hypocritical regarding the matter was the sneakiness in which I went about it. There were still some that I attempted to hide it from so I would keep that "saintly" persona about me. And of course, Deacon Dan had given me my first lesson in how to be sneaky with respect to church 'traditions.'

You know Jesus reserved his harshest criticism for the Pharisees—aka Chief Hypocrites. Those who were good about "putting on a show for others."

As I reflect on this situation, now hopefully with a little more wisdom than my spongy spine gave me back in 1971, I've concluded that we shouldn't be worrying about how far we can push the bar until it's wrong, rather we should strive in everything to want to be better than what we can be. God himself said, "I desire mercy not sacrifice." That's an attitude of the heart. For example, God cut King Hezekiah slack because they couldn't celebrate the Passover at the right time. But Hezekiah's heart was in the right place. (See 2 Chronicles, chapter 30 for the cool story!)

If there's anything we've learned about Jesus, it's that he was a man of principle. For instance, if a man lusts over a woman but does not touch her, he has still committed adultery. That's a principle. If we try to find a way around a law that we don't like, that's being a hypocrite—a legalistic hypocrite at that.

Me? I'm like the guy with the two sons in the Parable that Jesus used to make a point. One son when instructed to work in his father's vineyard said *"No"* but then changed his mind and did the task. The second son said, "Sure!" then changed his mind and did not do what he said he was going to do. Jesus said, *"Which of these did the will of his Father?"* His disciples answered the first son to which Jesus acknowledged that was the correct answer. (Matthew 21:28–32) That first son was me. But being me *always* means having to say, "I'm sorry." Hence, this book.

Bottom line—when a Christian is chasing justification instead of sanctification, which is the process of making oneself holy... or setting ourselves apart from the world by doing the right thing, that person is chasing hypocrisy. Do as I say, not as I do.

Maybe since you're reading my book you think I've finally figured it out. I published a book so I must know all the answers, right? Spoiler alert: I can't solve anyone's problems. All I have is memories and lessons that I've learned throughout my life. And guess what, I'm still learning.

Although I didn't know it at the time, I now know exactly when I became an alcoholic. The year was 1975. ZZ Top, that 'little old band from Texas' was headed for San Antonio to promote their new album *Fandango!* With an appearance on KTFM and a concert. All the area deejays received invitations to the release party that was going to be held at one of the local general aviation airports. There would be a festive atmosphere that included helicopter rides, music, lots of Tex-Mex and most importantly, barrels packed with ice and Lone Star Beer.

While I was surely interested in hanging out with Dusty, Billy, and Frank, I began to think of the free-flowing beer more and more. To the point where my mouth watered.

Wow! Pretty much all the beer I could drink AND the best rock and roll music in Texas. Worked for me. The problem was, I was focusing on the alcohol and NOT the event. In fact, as the date drew closer, I kept thinking more and more about the free beer.

People, when that happens – that is, dreaming about an adult beverage more than the occasion it is celebrating— then 'what we have here is failure to appreciate...' appreciate just how much of a trap is being set. One of the earliest and surest signs of addiction is thinking, dreaming, fantasizing about something near and dear to our hearts that isn't good for us. It can be alcohol, drugs, an affair, you name it. We only set ourselves up for future disappointment at best and catastrophe at worst. I know because it happened to me.

What makes matters even worse is that God warned us about such things through a man named James. *"But each one is tempted when he is drawn away by **his own desires** and enticed. Then, when desire has conceived, it gives birth to sin; and sin, when it is full-grown, brings forth death."* James 1:14-15 (NKJV, emphasis added)

When what we desire consumes our minds, we'll often do stupid things to fulfill those desires and consequently good things will not follow.

Jumping ahead a few decades to 2021 you get a clear picture of a man attempting this teeter-totter of a balancing act. My wife is quadriplegic, and I am her caregiver. When it comes to my present drinking challenges, I've been justifying it as self-medication for what I've been going through. Sounds good, works pretty well, but any way you cut it, I'm chasing hypocrisy. For the readers who say, why don't you do something about it? I am. And I have cut back. But as any addict will tell you, it's hard. Very, very hard to do.

+++

While this book is about one of my feet in the world and the other one in the church, you've probably noticed that one of my biggest struggles is drinking. However, there actually *WAS* a time when I didn't drink at all. Primarily because I didn't like the taste of beer. I had yet to experience a beer buzz. When I was at USAFA Prep School in Colorado, a bunch of us guys who couldn't get a date (heck, we didn't know anybody!) decided to hang out and 'drink beer.'

In 1966, the local car rental agencies in the Springs would rent Ford Mustangs to Prep School cadets for only $15 a weekend!! That was bargain basement prices even back then. So, a bunch of us rented one of those cool Mustangs and headed for a vacant area outside the Colorado Springs metro. Another rarity of the time was that the state of Colorado sold beer (3.2% alcohol content) to anyone 18 and over. Beer was beer as far as these guys were concerned. But to someone like me who'd never drunk, 3.2 might as well have been 10.2.

We parked on a deserted bluff and began drinking cans of Coors 3.2 that we had purchased on the way. Everybody was getting loose and having fun, laughing about our instructors and talking about girls. Not being litter conscious, and after consuming their beer, the guys would toss the empty cans out on the rocky ground and laugh as the clatter of the can hitting the gravel caught everybody's attention.

I had been sipping my beer, thoroughly NOT enjoying its taste and knew that I needed to toss my can out the window so the guys would think that I was… well… one of the guys. And that's exactly what I did. I tossed my almost full beer can on the hard ground and it landed with a THUD. You could have heard a pin drop followed by the guys shouting, "Noble, you idiot! What did you do that for?"

I refrained from telling them the real reason, just that I wasn't in the mood. But I think they suspected otherwise that I was not a fan of beer. In any case, they weren't impressed. Too bad my alcoholic tastes didn't remain so innocent. To make matters worse, I wasn't invited to the next 'guys night out' for the next beer-drinking extravaganza! Just as well. I wasn't impressed with their litter bug antics. It's never cool to throw beer cans out the window… empty OR full.

Thinking back on this memory, I wish I had known enough to establish the person I wanted to be rather than wanting so badly to be around the crowd and allowing them to influence me. I admit, all the foolish decisions I made throughout my life were of my own choosing, nobody twisted my arm or pressured me into them. I simply wish I had more sense along the way.

I hope you don't think when I'm talking in this way that all I have towards the life I've lived is regret. That's not the case. I've been honored and blessed with so many amazing experiences. The best way to describe how I really feel towards my shortcomings is this. They are like taking all 2,109 steps to the very top of the Sears Tower. But at the moment I finished that last step, exhausted and out of breath, I looked over to see Jesus with a raised eyebrow, "Did you realize there's an elevator?"

Yep, that's me, making it difficult for myself.

CHAPTER 4

PERSONA NON PERSONA: WHO AM I?

---

*"She glided around the classroom like
waves crossing the ocean and my 12-year-old heart
pounded whenever she floated past my desk"*

As I pursued a career in the Air Force, I never considered what consequences might lie ahead—war, injury, the traumatic events I might be exposed to. I simply pursued what I wanted to pursue. The same was true when it came to my radio career. I never thought about who I might have to become to be successful.

While the thought of meeting famous people and potentially becoming famous myself had crossed my mind, it never occurred to me what that might actually look like until I was living it out. As mentioned earlier, there wasn't too much thought about how this might collide with my faith.

Well, there should have been.

Fans of A.O.R. radio (Album Oriented Rock) expected their deejays to drop the names of the celebrities they hung out with and what happened during those events. It was all part of the on-air lifestyle. Nobody read the "Dear Abby" newspaper columns for cooking advice, they turned to that section to get the juicy gossip and advice on relationships. It was, and probably still is, the same with the radio. Of course, people do want to hear deejays talking about their close-to-celebrities lifestyle, but they also want to hear their passion for the music, or even a day in their life (if it's interesting), in the context of a warm, natural, and conversational presence delivered by someone who can make that experience relatable and compelling to the listener.

I wasn't cut out to be a shock jock like Howard Stern or a zany jock like Rick Dees. What I knew I was good at was being warm and friendly with a good sense of humor. So, I settled on just being myself, like Hal McLain, who was the midday host on KULF 710 AM. McLain was different. He was remarkable not because he was a showman, but because he always sounded warm and friendly, and I think people responded to his genuineness. He came across as a friend. Someone you wanted to hang around with or share a meal with. My goal was to be just like Hal McLain. Why?

He would tell stories about his life. There wasn't a bunch of hype or brags about who he rubbed shoulders with. He loved flying and he loved people. Best of all, he was an amazing storyteller, which is a great quality for someone on the radio. I could vicariously fly in his airplane or be with him anywhere he talked about because he was inclusive.

But, as mentioned, my radio persona would eventually collide and cause some rather conflicting moments with my faith.

+++

While on the topic of deejay personalities and faith, I'd like to take a moment to introduce you to Nick St. John. He was the evening deejay on KTFM San Antonio. And he was known for saying outlandish things on the air. This unforgettable incident had repercussions all the way up to Heaven. Well, almost.

KTFM had an agreement with Santikos Drive-In Theaters to play the station on the hundreds of car speakers available on their large lots. Theater goers could listen to the station until showtime when the audio would change to whatever was showing on the big screen. During this time, early evening during the warm summer months, Nick St. John was on the air. On one notably infamous night, he whispered loud enough over a song, but not too loud, "Free hot dogs at the snack bar. Free hot dogs at the snack bar."

He just made that up. There were no free hot dogs at the snack bar, but you couldn't tell the hundreds of people who heard that announcement otherwise. The station was left with honoring Nick's 'commitment.'

Nick was warned but, as he proved just one week later, sometimes the temptation is just too hard to resist, especially when it involves a laugh.

So, 7 days after 'hot dog' Friday, Nick St. John claimed that KTFM was the station that God listened to. As you can imagine, this was a little more serious than free hot dogs. Many people were offended, both believers and non-believers. So, he was reprimanded and told to apologize. The next night and during his apology Nick said he was sorry that he had stated over the air that "KTFM is the station that God listens to." He apologized profusely, paused for effect... then added, "But it *IS* the station that Jesus listens to."

The listener firestorm that ensued was a tough one to put out. Believers and non-believers wanted blood. So, management relented and fired St. John the next day. KTFM may not have been the preferred radio station in Heaven, so to speak, but it's safe to say that Nick St. John had a growing fan club who could scarcely contain their glee at what he had done.

Maybe this is one of the reasons I thought it was best to separate my faith and my airtime for most of my career.

+++

I was raised Catholic, attended parochial schools from fifth through ninth grade and learned early on that guilt can be a powerful tool in the hands of a sour old nun or bitter pastor. Allow me to take you back to a seriously parochial era Circa 1960.

The girls swayed to Frankie Avalon's 'Venus' on their transistor radios standing in line to confess sins. Meanwhile, Father Getoffamylawn would respond to the innocent confessions of pubertal eleven, twelve and thirteen-year-old kids, by shouting, "SPEAK UP!" Father Getoffamylawn was hard of hearing. On the other hand, Sister Mary Glum's hearing was acute. She could hear whispers in the back of the classroom. "Ugh! Can you believe she heard that??" Sister Mary G took aim at individuals who dared to test the hard-core mettle of Dominican nuns. In other words, "Don't talk back, yakety yak."

Oh, they weren't all bad, in fact, they weren't bad at all. They were very strict and meted out discipline frequently and 'generously', but a few rotten apples took aim at some of us when we were most vulnerable. One such nun was Sister Mary Monster (name dramatically changed to protect the innocent, which she wasn't). So, we called her Sister M&M. She was my eighth-grade teacher and rarely cracked a smile. She was more likely to crack a whip— like Sister Mary Stigmata aka 'The Penguin' in *The Blues Brothers* movie. "No-nonsense allowed!"

I had brought my new Boy Scout pocketknife to school to show it off. Its blades were sharp and glinted like darting minnows in a sun-bathed tidal pool. Well, apparently one glint hit Sister M&M square in her left eye, and she began to move slowly and methodically down my aisle.

I quickly placed the knife between my shaking knees, folded my empty and sweaty hands on the desktop and proceeded to act as if nothing happened. When she suddenly stopped next to my desk, I knew this situation might end badly.

"What do you have in your hands?" she asked.

In a slow, shaky and submissive voice; I replied, "Nuh...thing."

Just then my knees popped open, and the knife fell at Sister M&M's feet. She slowly stooped down and picked it up while fondling my knife in both of her hands. Admiring it as she did so. Then she glared at me, placed the knife behind her back and with her other hand, pointed directly at me, raising her voice, and proclaiming for all to hear, "YOU LIED!!!" (Well, not really. The knife melted in my kneecaps, not in my hands.)

I'm sure my eyes must have been the size of saucers as I stared at her, realizing me and my knife were done for. My 'gulp' got stuck in my throat, but I didn't dare cough to dislodge it. I'd been better off passing out on the floor than disrupting her Oscar moment. Clutching my knife, she then whirled like Darth Vader and dashed her way back to her TIE fighter desk. You could hear a pin drop... and... everybody looked at me...the 'liar'!

Life as I knew it was over.

Yes, guilt, when conscientiously applied in a parochial program of regularly applied accusations, can be most effective at changing a whimpering twelve-year-old with a knife into a mound of quivering Jell-o.

One of the 'good guys' was Sister Mary Peter. She was my sixth-grade teacher, and I had a nun-crush on her. All I could see of her skin were her beautiful hands and face. She was young and although covered from head to toe in a white and black habit (her gown that almost hit the floor) it wasn't enough to hide her shapely figure. She glided around the classroom like waves crossing the ocean and my twelve-year-old heart pounded whenever she floated past my desk.

If I had to pick one word to describe the religion of my youth, it would be 'guilt'. I was raised on guilt, which on the surface was good in the sense that I knew when I had done something wrong. Catholicism taught me the meaning of *Mea culpa, mea culpa, mea maxima culpa*. Those Latin words were branded onto my heart: "My fault, my fault, my most grievous fault." It didn't matter that Jesus died on the cross so that my sins were forgiven. I still had to feel badly about them.

A little guilt is good because we should recognize when we have committed offenses. The problem was, I felt badly, for like… my whole life!!

As a matter of fact, I still feel awful about my first lie. I even remember it like it was yesterday. I was six years old. My brother Larry was four. I scribbled something on the kitchen wall with a pencil and when mom saw it, she sat us down and demanded to know which of us was the guilty party. Since my brother wasn't very good at speaking yet, and couldn't defend himself, I said, "He did it!"

I absolutely knew I wasn't telling the truth, but mom punished my brother and I got off scott-free. Poor Larry looked at me with eyes that didn't know what just happened. But I did.

Fast forward to 1971 and contrast those early parochial experiences with my future wife Kay, at age seventeen, who gently persuaded me to read the Bible and study with her minister. I did and became convinced I was in need of a Savior. Jesus had entered my life. He saved me not with guilt but with Grace. This was a whole new kind of religion I was experiencing.

But as I grew older, married, and had children, I slowly fell from Grace and began a dance with the devil that would prove catastrophic in years to come.

+++

CHAPTER 5

THE SELF I SERVED

"Without realizing it, I was becoming a moral schizophrenic."

My radio career began in 1973. Technically 1972 if you count the year I spent at Columbia School of Broadcasting. Kay and I were busy raising the first of two daughters. Shari was born in Houston in 1972. Mandi arrived in '75, nine months after we moved to San Antonio.

I love my wife Kay so much and did not want to disappoint her in any way. I'm compliant; a pleaser, and I wanted peace in our home. What I mean by that is I wanted to live up to the expectation I believed my family had for me. I had all these ideas of what was expected of me as a husband, a father, a good church-going man even though no one had ever voiced these expectations. I was expected to provide a good life for my family and have a particular "profile" whenever I was around church people—especially Kay. She had high standards… higher than mine. On reflection, it's quite possible I failed to meet those standards but wanted her to think I had.

This chink in my Christian armor began to grow bigger with time.

To understand why my life split into two lives—it's essential to understand just how strong Kay's relationship with God was/is. Kay grew up a conservative Christian in a strict home, the third of five kids. Her father abandoned the family, moving to Northern California when Kay was eleven, which left her to be raised by her mother. The first time I laid eyes on him, he was in his casket. That was 1987.

The fact that her father deserted not only Kay but the whole family left permanent scars including trust issues that often showed up at the times I tried to be tender. So, basically, Kay was slammed by the most important men in her life – her dad and me. Her dad was dead, but I still had to deal with his abandonment, and Kay had to deal with my alcoholism. Had I put two and two together, I would have tried harder to quit my addiction.

When I was at home, I upheld the standards I thought Kay would be proud of; the respectable church-going husband and father. But when I got to the studio none of those parameters—or maybe better put "rules"—existed. I could just be me, or at least that is the lie I believed. It was the same old lie the Enemy has been feeding mankind since the beginning of time. "Can you really *not* do that? Surely it won't be as bad as you think."

I know, the Enemy had his foot in the door as I evolved into two people. Without realizing it, I was becoming a moral schizophrenic. The more I dabbled in both worlds, the more I found myself adapting to my surroundings—a chameleon of sorts. I could blend in wherever I found myself, which really meant I began to lose who I was without ever realizing it.

As a radio deejay, there were many invitations to concerts which usually included passes to the green room. The green room would be stocked with beer and wine. Aside from that, I was sometimes invited to the after parties which I willingly partook in and enjoyed. Hey, who wouldn't like schmoozing with rock stars and rubbing elbows with movie stars and celebrities? With enough beer and wine, I could pretend I was one of them. Someone once said, "Show me your friends and I'll show you your future."

Was that a future to aspire to? Honestly? Yes! I wanted the best of both worlds—the faithful husband and celebrity friend—but due to the moral conflicts, I could only truly exist in one. However, I was not yet willing to accept that.

For most people back then, the rock star lifestyle was made up of drugs, drinking heavily, partying, smoking marijuana, 'free' sex, and lack of sleep. Even though deejays weren't rocking out on stage with the band, most of them, including myself, dabbled in similar lifestyles, although I can honestly say I did not take drugs, saving myself for alcohol instead. My idol, China Smith (KWST), and a competitor I greatly admired, the legendary B. Mitchell Reed (KMET), are two deejays I believe may have had their lives shortened, possibly because of this lifestyle. They were both 56 when they died and both suffered from heart issues. While I had no personal knowledge of such behavior, it is undeniable that many in my profession die prematurely due to lifestyle choices like smoking, drinking, and drugs.

Around 1977, I began supplementing my radio income with an instructor position at Columbia School of Broadcasting. As such, my students were encouraged to be real but here I was a hypocrite, dipping in both worlds just didn't realize it. We'd go to church and sing about giving all to Jesus, Lord and Savior, then show up at work and do whatever.

This conflict was within my soul, so most of the time, things looked ok on the outside. In fact, there were even some shining moments. Take for instance, the 1977 nominations for Billboard Magazine Major Market AOR Personality of the Year Award. I was the morning host at KLOL Houston— 'Mother's Family.' KLOL was the local 'hippie' station, and 'Mother's Family' represented the tight-knit 'summer of love-Woodstock' vibe on the radio. So, if you listened, you were probably a hippie. Or you may have thought you were.

There were some real heavyweights in those nominations, including B. Mitchell Reed and John Records Landecker but, unbelievably, I won! I was a rookie, and I beat the best… or at least the judges thought so.

Nevertheless, winning that award went straight to my head. I was the guy in the Beach Boys' line from *Get Around*, "I'm a real cool head making real good bread." Mm-hmm. Not exactly a recipe for humility. Naturally, I didn't make 'real good bread.' But with this award, I thought I would.

+++

Allow me to briefly take you forward in time to the year 1985. We were living in California and Stephen F. Austin High School was hosting its 1965 twenty-year class reunion. I drank way too much because nobody was watching me, or so I thought.

God, of course, was watching me.

I had given the church we attended back in Houston a heads up that I would be in town. They asked me if I could lead their worship service. I accepted and looked forward to showing how I had grown as a Christian. Turns out the opposite was true.

I sure didn't plan on getting wasted at my high school reunion. Of course, I hadn't taken into consideration that if one drinks all night long, no amount of showering and mouthwash is going to get rid of the stinky smell of alcohol.

The next morning, following worship service, I noticed people were avoiding me, people I hadn't seen in years. They ordinarily would have been gathering around and hugging me. It was truly embarrassing. After church services, when I got in the car with my best friend David, I realized I was still buzzed from the night before and it was at that point it became clear that I had been balancing *one foot in the world and one foot in the church*. Sadly, at this very moment, BOTH feet were in the world. I had led worship under un-worshipful, selfish conditions – a sin of the highest proportion and I owned it.

I was a hypocrite. I hated it. Yet, as much as I hated it, there was part of me that came back for more… and more. This is no new struggle for Christians. The apostle Paul, who started out as a man named Saul that killed Christians, seemed to have the same kind of struggle back in his time according to Romans 7:15 *"I do not understand what I do. For what I want to do I do not do, but what I hate I do."* (NIV) Paul goes on later in this same chapter to acknowledge the struggle further. He too hated what he was seeing within himself, yet he realized there was no redemption or action he could do on his own to resolve this conflict. *"What a wretched man I am! Who will rescue me from this body that is subject to death? Thanks be to God, who delivers me through Jesus Christ our Lord! So then, I myself in my mind am a slave to God's law, but in my sinful nature a slave to the law of sin."* (v. 24,25)

Paul knew submitting himself fully to God, or NOT doing his own thing, was the only place he would truly find redemption. Unfortunately, I was not there yet.

+++

Whenever appearances were required at station promotions, the challenge of trying to meet the listeners expectations was overwhelming. If I heard it once I heard it a thousand times, "You don't look anything like you sound!"

That always bugged me even though I'd laugh it off and say, "I'll take that as a compliment." (Yeah, right) At the time, I had long, thinning blond hair, a reddish beard and mustache. Since I have a nice, baritone voice and no doubt sounded taller on the air ☺ they were probably expecting someone who looked like Dick Clark and was at least six feet tall. Oh well. Although it was a great chance to meet people, I never looked forward to hearing those comments.

Speaking of expectations of fans, back when Kay and I had only been married a little over a month we found ourselves at Houston Intercontinental Airport to pick up Kay's brother. We got to the airport early and drifted toward one of the many shops in the main lobby. Muhammad Ali's face caught my attention. He was on the cover of Time Magazine's July 26, 1971, issue wearing a chocolate brown polo shirt. I happened to look up at that moment and THERE HE WAS! Standing about 20 yards away in the lobby!! I muttered out loud, "He's wearing the SAME shirt as he is on the Time Magazine cover! Wow! Was that intentional?"

To which Kay replied, "Ya think?"

> *"Float like a butterfly, sting like a bee"*
> *– Muhammad Ali*

I quickly purchased the magazine and instructed Kay to go get his autograph. I, of course, was too embarrassed to do that. To my surprise, she grabbed the magazine and ran over to Ali and his three- or four-person entourage clamoring for his attention. As I caught up with her, I heard Kay exclaiming loudly, "Mr. Liston!! Mr. Liston!! Can I have your autograph?"

I thought I would die. Sonny Liston was Muhammad Ali's arch enemy in the ring. It was hilarious! I wasn't sure if I should roll on the ground in laughter or quickly grab her hand and escort her away. "Sorry about that, she's… confused. But can you still sign her magazine?"

To some extent, I could relate to this mistaken identity that Ali was dealing with at that moment. That's about how I felt every time a listener would meet me in person and say, "You don't look anything like you sound."

But unlike me, he seemed to play it off with less damage to his ego. (It always helps to be a tall, superstar hunk.) He chuckled while his entourage tried to suppress their laughter and amusement. Then being the gentleman he was, Muhammad Ali signed the cover of our Time Magazine, looked down at Kay and said, "Thank you! Nice meeting you."

It was an unforgettable experience. Ali floated like a butterfly, and WE were stung like a bee!

+++

When I was at home, I could be myself. (Besides, Kay didn't have much patience for egos.) I was with my wife and kids and life was normal. Or at least it seemed so. Those are the moments I know I was trying to be true to *myself*. But when it came to radio, I was trying to be *someone else*. I wanted to be accepted by my listeners and guests. As much as I started out modeling my style after Hal McLain, I soon forgot to stay genuine going for a quick one-liner or trying too hard to be funny when I wasn't.

Beer was tolerated in the house but unwelcomed, nonetheless. Whenever I took a cold one out of the fridge, I got the *evil eye*. So, I learned to be sneaky. Oh great, why didn't I figure it out back then that a sneaky alcoholic is two people?

Like the priests and nuns from my school days, I wasn't all bad. But if I wasn't who I wanted to be, and I wasn't quite sure who I wanted to be, what kind of person was I?

Well, I can go back to when I was ten years old. I had a Houston Chronicle paper route. My bike was fitted with a double wooden rack saddled across my back fender and it was full of papers. The Sunday paper delivery had to be divided into a couple of trips because I had over a hundred customers and the papers were heavy!

One Sunday morning, there was this homeless guy at the convenience store where my papers were dropped off. We started talking. It was the first time I had been exposed to a homeless person. His name was Thomas. He may have been drinking, he was disheveled, dirty, and smelly.

He asked if I had any money and I said no I didn't. He was talking about how cold it was and I said, "Well, after I'm done with my route, I could take you back to the house. Mom and dad can take you in."

We had a room upstairs that was open, and it didn't even occur to me that they wouldn't. I had faith in the love my parents had shown me and others. I brought Thomas back to the house and told my dad, "Hey dad, I told this guy he could stay with us since it is so cold outside."

Even though they looked like deer in the headlights when they saw him, my dad said, "Sure, come on in."

Deep down that is what my heart has always been—compassionate. Thankfully, God has generously allowed me to retain that quality—at least one personality trait that transcended both of my worlds.

Prior to 1973, and my first job in radio, I was in a little country rock band called *Treefrog*. It was Glenn Craig and me, and bass player Robert Oliphant. We played folk masses. I didn't become a member of a Bible church until right before I married Kay in 1971. (The music component of my career will be looked at in much greater detail in *Culture Jock II*)

Sometime that year before our wedding in June, I invited Kay to come to one of the 'Folk Masses' that were gaining in popularity across the parish. At the conclusion of the service, as Glenn, Robert and I were packing our guitars and amplifiers, Kay came up to the sanctuary rail and before she could say anything, the first words out of *MY* mouth were: "Hi honey, so how did I sound?" Compassionate, but with a big head.

I didn't start thinking about that for years. The emphasis shouldn't have been on ME immediately following the service. That shouldn't be the emphasis for any worship leader. When the focus is on ME there's always room for error... and inflated egos. Instead, the focus should be on God. She kind of pulled back but didn't say anything.

+++

My bandmate, Glenn, made the unfortunate decision of falling in love with a sixteen-year-old although he was twenty-three. They were intimate and her parents put an end to it.

In May of 1973, Kay and I moved to Bryan-College Station (about eighty miles Northwest of Houston) to take my first job in radio. I said goodbye to Glenn, Robert and *Treefrog*. The band was no more.

Within days of working at the station, I heard Glenn had taken his own life. I'll never forget the date because it was our second wedding anniversary, June 4, 1973. The band had broken up and he lost his girlfriend. Because I had just started work, I decided not to attend the memorial service. Looking back, I should have gone. I wish I had gone because he was my best friend but instead, I put my work first.

This was a trend I continued for much longer than I care to admit. Almost always making work (or surfing) a priority over everything and everyone else. As you can probably guess, this eventually caused a lot of problems in our marriage. If you were hoping for some lesson to take away from my story, it's this: Don't be that guy! I should have put Kay first.

+++

CHAPTER 6

BRACE YOURSELF!!!

At takeoff, instead of going straight up we went sideways. We missed hitting the power lines by less than a foot.

KORA AM/FM was a learning experience. Kay and I had only been married a couple of years. Our only bill was the fully furnished trailer, including utilities for $80 a month that Carolyn Vance, KORA AM and FM owner rented to us. I was getting paid $400/month (Hey, it was my first job in radio) Kay got a job as a secretary at Texas A&M. She was earning $525/month. So, Kay and I together were knocking down $925/month and renting a trailer for $80/month. It was the best cash flow of our lives.

I was working with some very talented people. Roy Garcia, the Program Director, had interviewed me for the job. He later went on to become Program Director of WUSN Chicago.

I always say that someone going in for a job interview has to be a little cocky. Although I told Garcia it would only take me a couple of hours to learn how to use broadcast equipment, even with evening jock Mel Levine teaching me 'the ropes', it still ended up taking two weeks to figure out what was going on. But Garcia must have admired my chutzpah because I got the job.

And although I went to CSB, Levine continued to share 'hands on' tips in a real-world environment. His input was invaluable. We also hosted a weekly cable TV show. It was fun! We played our guitars and discussed controversial topics on *our* show. CCIV offered local programming. It was the early days of cable television and I thought, "Wow, we've got our own TV show!"

It was a heady time for me and Mel.

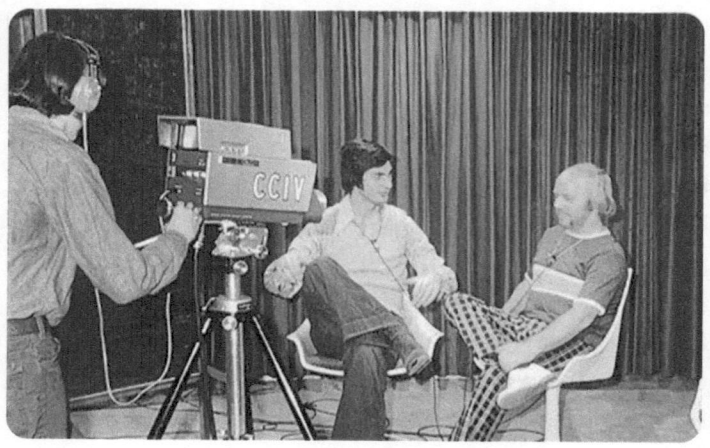

Prior to going on the air (and because we lived twenty feet away) I would spend a lot of my off time inside the station standing at the teletype machine. It was about the size of a water fountain and would shake out news and weather all day long. It had a roll of paper and printed out dot matrix news from the Associated Press. This would provide ample news and weather that we would rip and read on the air.

Because this was my first career job in radio, I was just thrilled to be at the station seeing things, hearing things, being around things. I wanted to learn and absorb everything that I could. I was so excited; I didn't even know when to *stop* talking during my overnight shift. My enthusiasm backfired on me once when a listener called in and sternly said, "Could you *please* shut up and just play the music?"

Oops! I suppose I had gotten a little too excited and chatty that day. Thereafter, it seemed like every program director I worked for reminded me that "Less is more." The lesson being, 'What you don't say won't hurt you.'

Richard Moore was the news person for the station. In his spare time, he played a zither which looks like a tiny piano without all the coverings, you can see all the strings and it's shaped kind of like a concert piano. Almost like a harp but it sounds different, more metallic, and it's cradled in your arms. It was great to be around people that enjoyed music at work and away from work as much as I did. In fact, we worked up a few songs together. It was fun and we even played a concert!

+++

KORA AM hosted very few concerts, but occasionally we got a star recording artist like Johnny Rivers ("Midnight Special" and "Poor Side of Town") who played at Texas

A&M, and Jerry Jeff Walker who performed at Bryan's Civic Auditorium.

Jerry Jeff Cuts Loose

Jerry Jeff Walker, wails a tune to a crowd of nearly 1,000 during his performance Friday night in the Bryan Civic Auditorium. The concert, sponsored by KTAM radio, also debuted the act of local talents Ken Noble and Richard Moore.

Mr. Bojangles was a hit song by the Nitty Gritty Dirt Band in 1971. It was written by Jerry Jeff Walker, a singer/songwriter from the Cosmic Cowboy, Austin City Limits era. Richard and I asked if we could open for the concert. JJW's management and the radio station gave their 'thumbs up'. Richard and I did the monkey dance thing. You had to be there, but it was really funny!

I remember we performed three songs for the opening. Although I can't recall what the first two songs were, I clearly remember closing with Hot Tuna's *Keep on Truckin'*. I was singing and at one point went into a real high pitched falsetto sounding like a cross between Steven Tyler and Tiny Tim. It was a blast! We even had a brief mention in the newspaper. Everyone went to the after party at Carolyn Vance's house. She was the station owner. I suppose we all expected to schmooze with Jerry Jeff Walker, but he showed up two hours late. Since it was already around midnight, Kay and I only stayed about fifteen minutes before leaving. Partying into all hours of the night wasn't really our scene.

KORA AM received new call letters in late 1973 and became KTAM, while KORA FM retained its well-known call sign.

I was at KTAM for just under a year. My philosophy was 'learn what you can' and move up because you're not going to make what you want in a small market radio station. The larger stations could pay more money because they made more money. The larger the market, the more money was paid to personnel. At least on paper.

But another dynamic I hadn't considered would also be at play —the bigger the market, the bigger the temptations.

+++

I sent a resume to KTFM in San Antonio and after being named new morning host in the Alamo City, we moved there in 1974. That's where I had my hot air balloon crash.

MEMO

TO: Ken Noble/KTFM Air Personality
FROM: Lee Taylor
DATE: August 12, 1975
RE: Public Affairs Project: Giant Balloon Ride
       from North Star Mall for Muscular Dystrophy

It is indeed an honor for me to announce that you have
been chosen from more than 100 San Antonio Disc Jockeys
to be the "air personality" to ride the Giant Hot Air
Balloon leaving North Star Mall (next to the marque)
hopefully going south over the city - 5:15pm Thursday -
August 14, 1975.

You should make plans to be at Chip Eichman's (Ike-man's)
office no later than 4:30pm. Chip's office is the North
Star Mall Merchants Association office above the Spiral
staircase near Frost Bros.

Please get with Tom Ortiz for "remote balloon equipment"
to be used for three on air cut-ins over KTFM (5:30p to
6:30p Thursday). Also, please follow thru with Stanli
Moore to see she logs these (no-charge) announcements and
the exact times you are expected to cut-in. Naturally,
you will also make arrangements with the KTFM on-air
personalities involved so that they too will know what
to expect from you. Furthermore, please see that
Anne Schiller schedules Muscular Dystrophy PSAs, Wednesday
and Thursday on KTFM, written by you, explaining that
you will be taking the Ride to create attention for a very
worthy project that needs total San Antonio support.

Thank you.

Lee

Copy: Public Affairs File   Tony Raven
       Ken Dowe   Tom Ortiz
       Trigger Black
       Anne Schiller
       Stanli Moore

Seriously. I was in a hot air balloon crash and survived.

In Texas, the winds frequently blow out of the south and in the afternoons, they can reach 15 to 20mph. So, rule #1 in hot air ballooning is: DO NOT LAUNCH IN THE AFTERNOON OR ANYTIME THE WIND IS OVER 5MPH.

It's best to launch a hot air balloon in the early morning when the air is calm.

I'm not sure why my female pilot friend went along with this, but I supposed she may have already been paid and probably needed the money. I was completely naïve. We're gonna go on a hot air balloon and I would make three call-ins to the radio station at seven hundred feet. Piece of cake, right? Not really.

At takeoff, with winds gusting from 10-20 mph, instead of going straight up we went sideways. We missed hitting the power lines by less than a foot, no exaggeration. Once we reached seven hundred feet we were just cruising. I made my call-ins to the station, and thought it was fun. But when I looked down there was nothing but mesquite trees as far as the eye could see and we were moving pretty fast. I turned to Bonnie, the pilot, and asked, "How are we going to avoid those trees when we land?"

She pointed to this postage stamp sized school and said, "Do you see that track and field? I have to get down there... NOW!"

Oh, great NOW she's worried about the wind.

She started letting air out of the balloon and we started descending quickly, although there was no sensation of falling. We were just on a smooth elevator so to speak. And besides, I was thinking what could go wrong? I enjoyed looking around at the clouds and feeling warm and fuzzy inside. I could imagine Tony Curtis and Natalie Wood from "The Great Race" sipping champagne from a hot air balloon. All so romantic. So peaceful. So fraught with disaster!

So, I'm looking around and the last thing I remember was her yelling, "BRACE YOURSELF!!!!"

"What???

We covered the last fifty feet in about two seconds and hit the ground hard.

I sprained my ankle on impact. The wind tossed the basket on its side, the balloon dragged us about a hundred yards. We were being thrown all over each other inside that basket. The dirt, dust, shards of flying dandelions, grass and bugs were shrouding our helpless bodies like so much debris following a tornado.

Thankfully a barbed wire fence put an end to our misadventure, ripping the balloon in half and letting all the air out before we finally stopped. Bonnie cussed up a storm. She was so angry. And me?

I was dazed and confused. And my ankle hurt really bad.

Her crew-van drove up and checked to see if we were ok. That was the last of it. If that had happened present day it would have made the evening news, but it was no big deal back then. Just another silly radio station promotion gone bad. Ha-ha. Yeah, seriously.

It wouldn't be the last crazy promotion I'd be subjected to in my radio career. But I will say, it should be noted as my most dangerous and terrifying. And never, ever, has there been a desire to get back into a hot air balloon.

+++

The overnight disc jockey at KTFM was in his early twenties, Jeff. As a young single guy, Jeff's pride and joy was his boat. He enjoyed taking it out on Canyon Lake whenever he got the chance. It was a very popular spot. I was always excited to hear about his adventures on the lake so there was no question in my mind when he asked if Kay and I would like to go skiing. He picked us up around 6am Saturday morning and we drove out to the lake.

It was a beautiful morning; the sun was glistening off the water's surface. Kay and I got into the boat while Jeff seamlessly backed it into the water. He captained the boat away from shore, found a good spot in the lake and shut off the engine. We were all excited to get this adventure rolling! Since the skis had to be put on in the water, I decided I would go first. I jumped off the boat but not far enough away from the motor. I landed on one of the propeller's blades and sliced the bottom of my foot wide open. Thank God Jeff had just turned the motor off. Luckily it was a freshwater lake and no sharks, otherwise, I was human chum! Blood seemed to fill the water like a *Jaws* movie.

They helped me back onto the boat and Kay wrapped it up tightly. Three minutes into our skiing adventure, we had to pack up and go home. I don't recall Jeff ever extending another invitation for us to join him on the lake.

During the day, my foot started throbbing a little bit but later that night it began throbbing more intensely. So bad that I decided to drive myself to the ER. Kay stayed home with the girls. As soon as the hospital staff looked at it, they said, "We're going to have to re-open your wound. It's already started to heal."

Who knows what it had inside of it? Parasites? Parameciums? Flesh-eating bacteria? It was red and swollen and now in need of stitches. The whole ordeal took an hour or so. I eventually healed with no major damage, thankfully.

The moral of the story? Know before you jump or look before you leap. But maybe even more importantly, when it came to San Antonio, attempts to take me out first by air and then by sea left indelible memories, not to mention a couple of scars.

+++

CHAPTER 7

LISTENERS: CHUMMY OR CHUMPY?

"What could I possibly see in a listener I had never seen?"

Judy Collins' hit song, *Both Sides Now* (written by Joni Mitchell) is somewhat cryptic, but basically invites the listener to look at the whole picture when going through life's difficult and challenging experiences. The song implies there are so many things we know so little about, that even when we think we know, or that we think we've got it made, we're not thinking.

> *"I've looked at clouds from both sides now,*
> *from up and down and still somehow,*
> *It's clouds illusions I recall;*
> *I really don't know clouds at all."*

When I first heard 'Both Sides Now' sometime in the late 60s, I had no idea what that song was about—it was just out there. Only as I have aged (and allegedly become more mature)—have I acquired some sense of wisdom... about the song and about life. Especially since I experienced the same "thinking I've got it made" principle in my life. Proverbs 16:18 was a prophecy that I went out of my way to fulfill: *"Pride goeth before destruction, and a haughty spirit before a fall." (KJV)*

I was pretty sure I knew it all and that after three solid years of broadcasting, the only way to go was up. I was on my way, baby, and the sky (clouds and all) was the limit!

Except I seem to have forgotten... 'What goes up, also comes down.'

It's like I was in a kayak in white water, headed for a steep, dangerous waterfall. This wasn't another crazy radio promotion; this was the actual course of my life. I just couldn't see it coming, but all the signs were there that something WAS coming.

In my forty-three-year career in radio, there were numerous temptations, primarily with beer and wine. Although the hard stuff was present in our industry, I was never offered it, nor would I have partaken in it if I had been. There was still some fire I just wouldn't play with.

I was also frequently solicited by listeners on the request line. Some wanted to meet me when I got off the air. And you know, it was tempting especially if the listener sounded attractive. But thankfully those conversations only went on for a few minutes because I always had somewhere else on the clock I needed to be... like the next commercial, news, traffic or weather break. That was my excuse to end the call.

In retrospect, I think the Holy Spirit was trying to get my attention. However, He would have needed to shout through a megaphone. That's how hard of spiritual hearing I was.

For example, I had a listener in San Antonio that was constantly calling me and coming on to me. (This was a morning shift 6am-10am) We never met but if we had she probably would have run away screaming because everyone was constantly saying I wasn't what they expected. LOL

Seriously, Linda was trying to get to know me. She didn't have to wait long. When my wife went out of town to visit family, I foolishly decided to give Linda a call off the clock. That's what a beer at 1pm will do to you. The conversation started to go somewhere it never should have gone.

As a radio personality, what shift you work can be directly proportional to what kind of trouble you can get into. Night shift deejays have more time to talk and consequently more temptations than day jocks. Morning people don't usually get into that kind of trouble— they just don't have the time while they are slaving away over hot mics to be part of any kind of mischief. They are awake, drinking coffee, interacting with other morning show actors like news and weather people, or traffic reporters, and so on. They are, in a word, busy. There is no time to follow ridiculous pursuits. Hence, calling Linda after work when I got home, seemed like a good idea.

But why? I was happily married with two great daughters. What could I possibly *see* in a listener I had never seen? Sadly, in some ways we men ARE alike. That sounds like an excuse, and maybe it is to a point, but temptation is just that because it is appealing on some level. Here was a woman giving me huge respect and attention. Something I did not necessarily get at home. Probably, largely due to what I said before, Kay had no tolerance for egos. That's no excuse but it is a possible reason. There was another component: Earlier I mentioned Kay's dad abandoned not only her, but her entire family when she was 11. If you don't think that caused some issues with men, then you're *really* not thinking. That doesn't absolve me, but it does add context.

In my mind, if I didn't have Kay's respect, well then, why not take a moment with someone who did respect me? There lies both the problem and the answer. To earn another person's respect, we need to forget ourselves, 'deny ourselves', and begin serving the other person in humility. That's what Christianity is all about—being humble not prideful. A humble husband shouldn't worry about whether their wife is or isn't giving them respect, instead they should be focused on loving their wife. That paradigm EARNS respect. It doesn't have to be demanded. I didn't get that lesson until much later in life. But thankfully, I did finally get it.

Now, back to Linda, two people who fantasize about each other based on their voices is a game plan for disappointment. Like a blind date where one or both parties have lied or exaggerated their age and looks among other things. Which are exactly how things played out in 1975 when I made that call. We talked about everything. She had a very sexy voice. And she kept playing up to me. Before I knew it, I was beginning to get aroused. Good grief, I finally said to myself, "WHAT THE HELL ARE YOU DOING, KEN?" I ended the conversation and, she never called me again.

Chalk one up for ego that could have led to disaster. But I wasn't out of the woods. Not by a long shot. I hadn't taken into account what I euphemistically call the *Napoleon Paradox* – just when you think things are getting better, they get worse.

But before we go there, I don't want you to think that the life of a deejay was all temptation—beer, alcohol, drugs, and lust. There is a lighter side to being a disc jockey that could be tons of fun. Literally, lots of tons.

For instance, I was asked if I wanted to ride an elephant in the circus parade. The Barnum & Bailey Circus was in town and to create publicity they invited TV and radio media personalities to ride elephants in the parade! WOOHOO! It was awesome. This was happening in downtown San Antonio. The lady in front of me was a popular TV news anchor. She didn't want to ride the elephant, but her co-workers coerced... uh... convinced her to do so. I think they knew it was going to be... interesting. ☺

Earlier that morning, it had rained quite a bit so there was still a lot of water in the gutters. The elephant in front of me walked through this puddle and sucked that thing dry like a shop vac. He lifted, then tipped back his trunk and showered the news anchor who was riding him with what looked like, for all practical purposes, a trunk full of elephant snot. She screamed like she had fallen into a pit of vipers. It was quite a sight to see her perfect blonde hair soaked with elephant snot. I mean, seriously, you don't see THAT every day.

We made the front page of the San Antonio Light the next morning.

+++

The next job I had was at KLOL in Houston. It was 1976 and the hometown boy had made good, riding back to town on a white horse! It had only been three years since I graduated from Columbia School of Broadcasting. My first shift was late night, 10pm-2am on 'Mother's Family' – a name that reflected the communal spirit of 'long-haired, freaky people' (a line from *Signs* by the *Five Man Electrical Band*). We relished being the hippie station and played a very eclectic blend of album rock. In fact, our music shelves contained about five thousand albums. Music knowledge was the key to having a successful program.

As I mentioned earlier, the amount of temptation you are exposed to as a radio personality can be directly proportional to the shift you work. Between the hours of 10pm and 2am, there are a lot of lonely people out there, especially in a city the size of Houston. Some of these people are nocturnal, some can't sleep, some are high on drugs or alcohol but many of them turn on the radio in the middle of the night. They use the radio much like many of us use a night light. We feel more secure.

The music we played was appealing to young women. A lot of that had to do with presentation. We did not shout or hype anything. We were deliberately conversational... even quiet by some standards and we tried to cultivate a bond with each listener whether they listened in their bedroom, bathroom, car or while exercising and so on.

I suppose it was for this reason that I had a listener frequently call and try to get to know me. Because I was working late nights, I had a little more time to have a conversation with this woman we will call Sharon. This young woman was divorced and made no secret of that. She convinced me to meet her when I got off the air one morning at 2am; I foolishly accepted her offer.

Forget the fact that I was married to the most wonderful, beautiful woman on the planet, I don't know why I did it. I regretted it and still do. It was a very bad decision. I showed very poor judgment and without going into any details let's just say I was unfaithful, and I regret that with all my heart. I have confessed that sin to my wife and that wasn't exactly a picnic either.

I should have remembered mom's advice: "Don't hang out with the wrong crowd because you'll become the wrong crowd."

People make mistakes. We ask ourselves, "How far can I go before I cross the line?" Then, most of the time, if we have determined that we've crossed the line, we vow not to do it again. As Christians, this should not be the case. I'm not saying Christians are perfect and will never make mistakes. I'm a *perfect* example that this is not true! What I'm saying is that as Christians we must acknowledge there is a difference between mistakes and sins. Mistakes are bound to happen. But sin is what we specifically choose to do of our own free will. Actions which take us out of God's Will and plan for our lives.

As Christians, instead of asking ourselves, "How far can I push the bar?" We should instead ask ourselves, "Am I living a life aligned with Christ?" This is the issue that I faced. I would go to church and hear about *how* to live for Christ.

> *"And now, dear brothers and sisters, one final thing. Fix your thoughts on what is true, and honorable, and right, and pure, and lovely, and admirable. Think about things that are excellent and worthy of praise. Keep putting into practice all you learned and received from me—everything you heard from me and saw me doing. Then the God of peace will be with you."* Philippians 4:8-9 (NLT)

There were Sundays when I'd get pumped up over a great message, and then walk out the door and immediately forget what I had heard. I knew what was right and wrong but somewhere along the way my conscience would get switched off and I would instead go with my feelings in the moment. It's not something new, "Moral memory lapses" happened quite often throughout the Bible—Eve, Samson, David, Saul, and countless others. Each of them, including myself, knew what was right, knew what was expected of them according to God's Word and decided to be like Frank Sinatra who sang *"I did it my way."* At which point, we deceived ourselves into being okay with doing something harmful. Talk about a prescription for disaster!

Was I a role model Christian or a hypocrite? To some extent, some might argue that we are all hypocrites at one time or another. We're all human and imperfect. But, I think, being a hypocrite is when you continually do things that you know God would not be pleased with by ignoring our heart, which is being guided by the Holy Spirit to direct our steps. I was not a role model Christian, but I pretended to be one. I could flip on the Christian jargon as if it was a switch in the studio. Music... *switch*, commercial break... *switch*, news... *switch*, Christianese... *switch*, shop talk... *switch*, communion... *switch*... you get the idea.

To feed my ego even more, being a hometown guy was like 'local kid makes good' status. Kay and I both grew up in Houston and now here I was working for this local, very hip, and popular radio station. Could it get any better? Yes, it could! We'd get invited to all the events and people's homes at church which of course had my ego basking in delight. I fed that image and it felt good to be noticed, to be enjoined with community leaders who oversaw important projects that involved city, county or even state relationships. Hey, I was hangin' with the mayor or even the governor at times. Heady stuff. But I was only kidding myself that I was a good role model.

+++

In 1976 I was invited to hang with the Program Director and a former member of Fleetwood Mac for what can best be described as a brief encounter with dress codes. KLOL Program Director Jackie McCauley invited me to join her and ex-Fleetwood Mac singer/guitarist Bob Welch for lunch. He was in town for an interview and to promote his new solo album, 'French Kiss' featuring his solo single, *Sentimental Lady*. He had written the song as a member of

Fleetwood Mac and it is indeed on the Mac's 'Bare Trees' album.

We headed out to the fashionable southwest side of Houston to the Westheimer District and approached a famous local eatery (that needs to remain unnamed here, sorry). I was wearing a t-shirt. Bob Welch was wearing a black satin shirt with long sleeves. Jackie had a nice pullover, but we were all wearing jeans. Our clothes were clean and quite honestly, we looked fashionably hip. But that wasn't good enough for the restaurant which had a dress code. Wear a tie or get turned away and die an embarrassingly slow death, right?

They turned us away.

Had they known it was Bob Welch formerly of Fleetwood Mac, it's likely they might have made an exception. We laughed it off and had lunch instead at the Hobbit Hole. A popular upscale eatery in the same area. Needless to say, all we could talk about during lunch was how we had been summarily dismissed like so much 'riff raff'. (Say it with a Brit accent and you'll feel snooty ☺) LOL

+++

One of the cool things about being in radio is that we—those of us who are on the air—can create our own alias or *nom de guerre*. For example, a couple of the deejays at KLOL had the coolest, catchy names. The guy who worked 6pm-10pm was Jack Smack, he did the 'Jack Tuck' where he tucked the listeners into bed. "Ahh. That's so sweet." Emile

Forreal, a name that rolls off the tongue so easily, was the overnight jock.

I think the coolest name ever was a part timer I had immense respect for, Ace Paladino. Ace was born a stutterer. He stuttered anytime you talked to him but on the air he was flawless. How does that happen? On air his star was shining, he was a great guy with a wonderful voice who sounded so good on the radio.

Then there was Trigger Black, my program director at KTFM in San Antonio. His real name was Gary, but on the air, he became 'Trigger.' Cool as cool gets.

When you're in radio you can become the person you want to be and having a catchy *nom de guerre* or an alias was part of the plan, even fun. There were some people who were exactly as they were on the air and then there were some who were nothing like they were on the air. (Me for one!) And then there was Charlie Tuna. Here was a guy who was ridiculously different from his on-air persona, but likeable as both. Being Charlie Tuna was like being a superhero on the air... and at home, more like Clark Kent. In my honest opinion, he was the best at what he did of anyone I have ever known in radio.

One could argue that having an alter ego for on-air purposes is a dynamic that can lead to moral schizophrenia. Radio gave us the chance to be the person we needed to be for our listeners. That's the fun part of being a deejay—becoming someone who you know you'd like to be but for whatever reason, you lack the confidence to be that person... until you're on the air! Yeah, I can see how the person I wanted to be may have thought that being appreciated, respected... heck, even adored on the air, was license to do things I never would have done outside of broadcasting.

And that's the lie.

+++

CHAPTER 8

BUSTED FLAT IN CHICAGO?

*"Rock had AC/DC's 'Big Balls';
Disco had glitter balls."*

"That's no lake. It's an ocean!"

I left KLOL Houston in 1977. Our family had driven up to Chicagoland—Kay, me, and our daughters Shari (5) and Mandi (3). I was taking over the morning position at WLUP FM 98, The Loop—a new rock station in Chicago. After winning the AOR (Album Oriented Rock) *Major Market Air Personality of the Year* award a few months earlier while at KLOL Houston, I used it to leverage what I thought would be a wave of success… if you want to call a job that only lasted seven months successful. More on that in a bit.

When we saw the lake, we were completely blown away, it was amazing. Lakeshore Drive is at the water's edge and separates downtown from Lake Michigan. It's an awesome highway with stunning views. And it had a sandy beach, real waves, and surf with white foam. In the winter it was not unusual to see ten-foot waves whipped up by 30-40mph winds howling out of the north and pounding the shoreline. In fact, Lake Michigan at times looks more like a giant washing machine in the heavy-duty spin cycle. In a cold winter, the ice can freeze up to two miles out. You can't see any blue water unless you're in one of Chicago's high-rises. For all practical purposes looking out over a frozen Lake Michigan is like looking out over Jupiter's ice moon, Europa.

The city has an amazing transit system— the CTA (Chicago Transit Authority) utilizes Amtrak, the 'L' (L is for Elevated train), buses and lots of cabs. Factor in Lyft and Uber and, nowadays, there's no excuse for not getting around this fascinating community.

Our hotel was waiting for us downtown Chicago, just a few blocks from the Hancock Center. We were there for a couple of weeks before we could find an apartment. But searching for a place to live in the Windy City is expensive! Everywhere we drove we had to pay a fee to park our car because it was in the downtown area.

This photo was taken shortly after we purchased our Skyhawk in 1976.

Five dollars here, ten bucks there. Before we knew it, we were coughing up $40-$50 a day just to park our Buick Skyhawk as we looked for an apartment. Nobody had free parking. Our car was as useful as a three-thousand-pound millstone around our necks. So, we put it up for sale.

We ended up finding a two and a half flat apartment in the Near North area. I commuted by bus to the prestigious John Hancock Center. At ninety stories, the JHC, as it is affectionately called, is one of the tallest buildings in the country. Our radio station was located on the thirty-seventh floor.

I went up to the roof once with the Chief Engineer. We were outside checking on the Loop's ginormous antenna. There are forever views from the top. It was like I was in orbit or something. I could see the curvature of the Earth... mm-hmm. (Well... almost.)

Because my shift started at 6am, I would catch the 36 Broadway metro bus around 4am. The only people hanging out at that hour were drunks, cops and a wide assortment of pimps, prostitutes, and drug dealers. How was I going to wait for my bus every morning and deal with some possibly dangerous street people?

I had an idea!

Let's see. I was from Texas, so I had a cowboy hat, cowboy boots, and Wrangler jeans. So far, so good. I also had a long McCloud-type corduroy jacket with fringe. If I slipped a Colombian *ruana* over my head (because it was dang cold in late November) and I copped a cocky attitude, I just might be able to do this! (Never let 'em see you sweat!) By the way, a *ruana* is basically a poncho/wrap made from llama wool. Think Jon Voight in *"Midnight Cowboy."*

With my reddish beard and mustache, I fit right in with the crowd. And that's what I wanted to do. I did not want to show up in a suit or wearing polo shirt and slacks to catch the bus. Those polyester vestments had "Mug me and beat me to a pulp" written all over them. I was different enough that they accepted me as one of their own and left me alone. I'd show up and they'd say, "Yo cowboy, how you doing, bro?" One of the ladies would chime in, "You wanna date?"

"Uh...no thanks. Maybe next time." (What else do you say to that?)

We were only there for seven months, so going incognito was convincing and thankfully didn't last that long.

We arrived in November, one week before Thanksgiving of 1977. It was cold, and snow was in the forecast. My program director Jay Blackburn was also from Texas which is why I think he liked me. He called everybody Bubba. I had been there for 3 days when he said, "Hey Bubba, why don't you come over to our house for Thanksgiving."

What I heard was Thanksgiving *dinner* but what he meant was something different. Well, I heard the part about coming over at six o' clock. Sounded a little late for the traditional meal. Back home we usually sat around the table around 2pm.

Their house was outside the downtown area. We walked up to the door and knocked. Jay answered the door, stoned beyond redemption, and there was a cloud that any pilot would have to file an instrument flight plan to punch through. The marijuana smell rolled out like fog covers San Francisco and enveloped us. I looked at Kay and she looked at me waving her arms in desperation to not let the pot smoke smother the girls.

I handled it by saying, "Hey Jay! We can only stick around for a little bit." (He *was* my boss after all.)

It was at that time I remembered he said stop by for *dessert*. Kay looked at me and said rather loudly and with an unsettling amount of satisfaction, "You didn't listen, did you?"

We walked in and various members of the staff were sprawled around the living room reclining on couches, La-z-boys, and the carpet. They all looked stoned as well. There were fossilized turkey bones on the table. We were literally there for only five minutes. We had to "get going". Only we didn't really have any place to be, and we still hadn't eaten our Thanksgiving dinner.

So, we went downtown.

It started snowing and the Magnificent Mile was picture perfect but deserted. Thankfully, we found a corner café that was still open with chalk-writing on the window that read: "SERVING THANKSGIVING DINNER WITH ALL THE TRIMMINGS." We hopped into the café and shook off the cold. We were their only customers and when we told this grandmotherly waitress with a careworn face that we had come in from Houston, she treated us like her own family. She brought us the feast, the trimmings and for dessert pumpkin pie with a dollop of whip cream… on the house!

It turned out to be one of the best thanksgivings ever. It was great!

The overnight host at the Loop was Garry Meier. But back in 1977, he was known as Matthew Meier. He was ridiculously funny. I know that because we did a minute or so deejay-banter-thing during the shift change at 6am. He also published an in-house comedy sheet called 'The Planet.' It was filled with one-liners and irreverent comments about many of the staff. This is the same Garry Meier who went on to work with Steve Dahl who became a superstar radio personality. In fact, they both did.

Dahl and Meier did a thing back in July of '79 called *Disco Demolition Night* where they piled up disco records donated by the thousands of fans who came to watch the fireworks. Entrance that night to the White Sox and Tigers game was only ninety-eight cents (to promote 98FM the Loop) and a donated disco record. They were piled as high as the Bee Gees voices in *Saturday Night Fever* at Comiskey Park, home team ballpark for the White Sox.

So why all the passion against disco? Well, for many during that era, if you loved rock, well, then "Disco sucks." Two different lifestyles—rock had fringy clothes; disco had shiny shirts. Rock had AC/DC's *Big Balls*; disco had glitter balls. You get my drift.

I watched Dahl blow up all those records on the national news on TV followed by Loop fans cascading out of the stands and onto the playing field. There was fire. There was mayhem. There were security guards with frozen faces. There was smoke and a thick haze over the infield. It looked like a scene from *Apocalypse Now*. ("I love the smell of burnt records in the morning!") And I suppose Comiskey Park and White Sox management were having cows. Meanwhile, I was like, "Wow that was a really great promotion explosion!" Steve Dahl had ended up replacing me when I left the show June 30, 1978. I was impressed and knew he was going places.

Dahl and Meier became instant national celebrities.

+++

Easter fell on March 26 of 1978 and there was an ice storm that started the night before. The low overcast cloud layer was down to about four hundred feet, hovering halfway up many of the towering Chicago skyscrapers. That cloud deck was where the storm was taking place. Every window above the overcast had ice on it. These building windows are huge, maybe five feet wide by ten-foot sections. As the temperature rose throughout the morning, these five by ten-foot ice sheets would slide off the windows and when they hit the ground it would sound like bombs going off, reverberating throughout Chicago's high-rise canyons.

My family and I didn't know anything about this. We went downtown on the bus, and they had the area taped off. I, foolishly, said, "Hey, how bad can it be... surely it's okay? We'll just be careful to dodge these ice sheets." Seriously? I said that?? Well, yes, I did. Back then I had a sponge for brain matter. We ducked under the yellow tape, clutched the girls' hands, and ran to the restaurant because, "By George' it's Easter and we're gonna eat out!". There were two ice sheet bombs that fell during that run through the downtown 'no man's land'— it was like a charge scene from *Sergeant York*.

The restaurant was happy to see us because not everyone was as dumb as us to run under the tape.

The Loop was owned by Terry Chess; one and the same of Chess Records fame and fortune. They produced hits for Chuck Berry, Muddy Waters, Bo Diddley, the Flamingoes and more. Shortly, after I started working for the station, it was sold to Heftel Broadcasting.

As soon as I found out, I knew I needed to apply for other jobs because it was always the morning show guy who was let go first. This was how the radio business worked. When a new owner bought a station, they would often bring in 'their' people. They might not, but I didn't want to chance it.

My dream was to get to L.A. so what better time to send out some tapes and resumes? It paid off. I was hired at a soft album rock radio station, KPOL FM in Hollywood. I was going to be an evening host. We had five people who ran the entire radio station.

The actual move to L.A. went like this—they paid for it.

Mayflower showed up with their truck. They packed everything and loaded it and they left. All we had to do was tidy up, vacuum our flat, get to the airport and fly to L.A. One of the smoothest, easiest moves I have ever experienced. The only difficulty was… my surfboard. It wouldn't fit in the trunk and the cab didn't have a roof rack. So, we ended up sliding it through both back, side windows.

The cab looked like it had wings—a giant, overweight canary.

We carefully drove to the airport so as not to clip any cars due to the surfboard, checked in and flew to LA. My brother, Larry, lived in Marina del Rey so he picked us up at the airport. Coolest cross country move ever! He graciously invited us to stay with him in his apartment as long as we needed.

+++

Other than surfing in a hurricane (Chapter 3) I haven't talked much about it up to this point, but for me, moving to Southern California was like a hiker headed for the Appalachian Trail. Surfing was my love language and Southern California was the mecca of surfing in the United States!

I had first learned how to surf, and fell in love with it, growing up in Houston less than an hour's drive from Galveston. For my eighteenth birthday, I was excited to receive my first surfboard. Of course, I was a little less excited when I realized I would have to share it with my younger brother, Larry. (Thanks Dad!) But we still had so much fun taking turns riding those smallish but quite enjoyable Gulf Coast waves that it didn't matter. Whoever wasn't riding would cheer the other on!

+++

Once home from the Academy, I needed to get caught up on my surfing. It was February 1967. The waves at 37th Street in Galveston were small but beautifully shaped and there was an offshore wind feathering the waves just as they broke. Air temperature was 48 and the water temp near 60. BUT… there was a 'NO SURFING', 'SWIMMERS' ZONE' sign in the water. Of course, nobody else was surfing and there wasn't a swimmer in sight. Hey, who in their right mind would be swimming in this chilly water in February?

I disregarded the sign, jumped in, and paddled out. It was a lot of fun for about ten minutes until the burp of a siren from the Seawall rudely interrupted my surf session. The Galveston County Sheriff was waving at me to come in. "What????" I said to myself, "You've got to be kidding me!" After nervously paddling in, the Sheriff handcuffed and arrested me for 'Surfing in a swimmer's zone'… in February. They confiscated my surfboard, finger-printed me, and locked me away in the county jail. I was cold, dripping wet and angry… mostly at myself. They allowed me to call Dad who couldn't come get me until after work. I spent the day in jail. The guy next to me in the tank said, "What are you in for… burglary, theft, assault and battery?" "Me?" "Nah. Surfing in a swimmer's zone." The guy looked at me like a chicken looks at a card trick.

The worst part of this? They held onto my board for two weeks. Ugh!

+++

Now, a dozen years later in Southern California, I was reunited with Larry and our passion for surfing. We took full advantage of the many nearby hot surfing spots before and after work and on days off. Kay wasn't that interested in going just to watch us surf—an early sign that my priorities were out of whack. "Hey Sweetie, wanna come watch me surf?" Oh man, I can't believe I was so dumb.

While we're on the subject of 'catching the stupid' as newsman Rob Carson is fond of saying, this story takes the cake... the wedding cake, that is.

Kay and I were married June 4, 1971, in her mom's apartment. We weren't permitted to have our wedding at the church building because I was a divorcee. I'd rather not go into why we couldn't be married in the church right now. Well-meaning people have strong opinions on both sides of this issue. And that's not what this book is about. But I will say that my first marriage was short lived. Six months, no kids, I got the bills, and she got the furniture. It was a sad moment in my life. I later found out she could not have kids; I can't even imagine how my life would have turned out without kids as my children have had an interesting way of spotlighting the areas where I needed it the most... maturing. Kay and I had two amazing sons and two awesome daughters.

On our wedding day, we went to the Flagship Hotel located over the water on a pier in Galveston. It was a very nice location and we planned to stay there for our honeymoon. As I packed the car, thinking about this hotel on the beach,

I began to paint a picture surrounded by amazing waves. What if the surf was really great and I didn't have a board to ride it? As Mr. Bill would exclaim, "Oh noooooooo!" That to me seemed like it could ruin the honeymoon. (Well-spoken by Mr. Sponge Brain)

I decided I should take my homemade surfboard to prevent such devastation. After all, I was getting married, going on my honeymoon, and might even get to catch some waves? What could be better? Maybe I should have collaborated a bit more with my beautiful new bride on what might make this her dream honeymoon. (I'd really love a do-over on that one ☹)

The surfboard was strapped to the roof and the car was parked outside the hotel. I didn't want to carry a surfboard into the hotel as that seemed like it might be crossing the line a bit or inviting criticism (Ya think?) The next day when I ran out to get the board and catch some waves; it was gone!

I could not understand why anyone would want to steal a homemade surfboard, but it was nowhere to be found. To this day, whenever I tell this story, 99.99% of the listeners say I deserved it. The other 0.01% called me names I won't repeat in this book. It took me a while to accept that they were right – one hundred percent of them.

+++

Back to the future of 1978, and aside from letting us stay with him, my brother also let us use his car while we were living with him in the Marina. Larry was a graphic artist at the time and did almost all his work at home. So, borrowing the car was not a big deal.

However, there was one very important consequence of selling the car back in Chicago. We would have had to take the bus to go to church on Sunday mornings. That became problematic when I was asked to host Sunday brunches at a local restaurant and grill. We needed the extra income it brought in. More importantly, I worked six days a week and Sunday was my only day off. For these reasons, we didn't attend any church services our entire seven-month stay in Chicago.

As I look back, I wonder if not going to church during this time helped cement my future 'one foot in the world, one foot in the church' mentality? I don't think it helped me spiritually, nevertheless we agreed to search for a church and a new car once we were settled in California.

When we began looking for an apartment, it was discouraging from the get-go. There were signs all over Santa Monica that read: "No pets! No kids!" Are you kidding me? After searching all over, we finally found a place, about two miles from the ocean, that 'allowed' children. "Thank you so much! You'll be glad to know our kids don't bark, don't bite and we take them for walks in the park." LOL

The "no kids" policy was ultimately changed during the 80s… about the time that *yuppies and dinks* who had occupied a significant percentage of California's population began having kids. Imagine that!

* "Young Upward Professional People" and "Dual Income No Kids"

+++

Once we found our new home (where children were welcome) we enrolled the girls in school. By the time 1980 had rolled around, we were living in a duplex in Westchester... about a quarter mile from LAX's parallel runways 2-5 right and 2-5 left. Good grief it was noisy, especially on Sunday evenings when every plane on the planet came home to roost.

We had to move and a home builder in beautiful San Clemente was offering great deals on new condos—a thousand dollars down for a three-bedroom condominium with an ocean view. We jumped on it and ended up with our first real home. Only problem was it was sixty-six miles each way to work. Oh well, a place like that was worth the commute... or so I thought.

The negatives of an epic commute take a while to show up. For one thing, I would get 'freeway buzz'. That's what I called it. My entire body would shake or vibrate for about thirty minutes after coming home... akin to riding a motorcycle over a long distance. It was a crazy feeling and more importantly I didn't want to be approached by anyone until it wore off. And of course, she who was waiting for me to come home didn't appreciate the lack of attention. Kay deserved better.

Not only was there freeway buzz, but I had no desire whatsoever to go anywhere, especially on the weekends and if the surf was good, everything else was planned around my need to be in the water. Not good. Selfish? Yes. And isn't selfishness one of the building blocks of hypocrisy? It was for me.

San Clemente was a surfer's dream overlooking one of the greatest breaks in the world—Lower Trestles. All during the 80s, I would surf there. I'd do the dawn patrol if I could, or I would surf on Saturday and Sunday before church then be home before Kay and the girls even got up. We'd hit the beach about four thirty in the morning, me, and a couple buddies.

In all, for twenty-five years, I was a passionate surfer and I saw it all.

Sharks would occasionally come a little too close for comfort. We always went in groups because getting mauled by a shark doesn't hurt as much when you have friends around, right?

I remember being a couple of hundred yards away from the shore one day when I saw a whale with her calf surface between me and the shore. That was amazing! I didn't dare get any closer though. Of course, there were always the occasional dolphins and seals as well. Dolphins were nice to spot, but if you saw a sea lion pop its head out of the water near you that was a clear sign it was time to move away. They were not fun to be around. They're like the bulldogs of the ocean. They have incredibly sharp teeth and can be intimidating.

Occasionally, I would drive up to Malibu and surf Malibu's 3rd Point – also one of the best point breaks in the world which of course meant it was always crowded. In the summertime, there could easily be a hundred surfers sitting in the water waiting on their turn to catch a wave. Since these waves were one person waves there could often be a lot of waiting. Catching one was a combination of jostling for position, luck, and skill.

But there's one unusual summer day which I remember more than any of the rest. It was hot, really hot, and this guy was surfing naked! He was the most obnoxious guy ever. I wouldn't surf naked but, if I had, I would have at least been low key. Not this guy! He was yelling at people and being so loud. Maybe he wanted people to notice him?

Because Malibu is a point break, the waves took surfers right along the shoreline as they wrapped around the point. So here was this obnoxious, naked guy riding the wave probably fifteen yards away from everyone sitting on the beach. To quote David Niven from the 1974 Oscars show quipping over a live streaker just as he was about to introduce Elizabeth Taylor, *"Isn't it fascinating to think that probably the only laugh that man will ever get in his life will be by stripping off and showing his shortcomings."* That was SoCal for you.

At one point, I ended up joining the Malibu Surf Club which was a longboard association. I loved to wear their red satin club jacket around town with "Malibu Surf Club" in white letters on the back. "Hey man, look at me. I'm a surfer!" Cool, huh? Yeah. No ego issues there at all.

+++

But, as they say, all good things must come to an end. In 1989, I decided it was time to set aside my passion for surfing the moment I realized I was about to be the father of a boy! Some would argue that I could take the kids surfing. What better father/son moment than learning how to surf, right?

Surfing was an escape for me, nothing but me and the waves. I decided to set aside my passion for surfing and exchange it for a passion to be a dad. There are a ton of great choices for dads and sons to share with each other in SoCal other than surfing. And we took full advantage of them. Besides, we spent plenty of time at the beach during our time in San Clemente. Kenny, Jr. was completely happy building sandcastles and playing with his bucket and shovel. And Kay was more than happy to come along because she knew I would be with her and that made her happy. And that made me happy.

It was a good decision to set down my surfboard and 'pick up' Kenny Jr. in the summer of 1990. I know I'm often hard on myself for all the boneheaded decisions I have made throughout my life, rightfully so, but this… I know this was a really good one! Never once have I regretted choosing to be a father instead of a surfer.

I haven't been on a surfboard since. And I'm okay with that. One might ask, well, if I could give up something I was so passionate about, why is giving up wine so very hard? Good question. And I don't know the answer to that.

+++

CHAPTER 9

L.A. PART ONE— COWABUNGA!!

"Her husband was VERY JEALOUS!
And he wanted me... DEAD!

So, where were we? Oh yes, 1978-82. "Kenny, that's k-p-o-EL-fm." Program Director Jack Popejoy welcomed me to Southern California and taught me how he wanted the call letters to be announced over the air.

CULTURE JOCK

"Okay, I think I got it. k-p-o-EL-fm."

Wow! What a move. We left a hot, humid Chicago and three hours later we were in cool Los Angeles on June 30, 1978. Now THAT's how it's done! Thank you, Mr. Popejoy, for giving my family the easiest, stress-free move ever! Our furniture showed up about two weeks later just as we were moving into our new apartment.

KPOL was a great place to work. We all had 'live', three-hour shifts followed by three-hours of voice tracked (taped) content. And for a couple of hours every day around lunch time, all five of us including Program Director Jack Popejoy, morning hosts Jim LaFawn and Neil Ross, and midday host Mike Sakellarides would gather at a round table like knights and squires discussing the latest battle plan to win the next ratings 'tournament'. Ratings came out every quarter. We also talked about life, politics, music, and each other. It was a magical time in my career. For the first time, I felt like I was actually contributing to the success of a radio station. I was in a group that was larger than the sum of its parts. We all wanted to make the sound that came out of the speakers better! And the cool thing? Our opinions and suggestions mattered.

But occasionally there's a dark side to radio. Remember, I was broadcasting live for three hours beginning at 6pm. And by the time I hit the air, I would have already recorded my three-hours of voice tracks. Which meant I would be on my way home soon after 9pm, but recorded breaks known as voice tracks kept up the illusion that I was still there for another three hours. That system may have saved my life.

A guy called me one evening before 9pm and said, "Hey, you're not who you say you are. You're Lee 'Baby' Simms." (Simms was a local well-known deejay).

I said, "You must be mistaken. My name is Kenny Noble."

He didn't buy the truth, but instead accused me of 'talking' to his wife through the radio. That's worth repeating. He accused me of 'talking' to his wife through the radio. She must have liked my voice or something. I'll never know, but for whatever reason, her husband was VERY JEALOUS! And he wanted me… DEAD! He said he was coming over to the station when I got off the air and would settle things then. I called the police, and they parked a squad car out front to keep an eye on things.

I usually left the station around 9:30pm. But my voice tracks kept the show going until midnight. Since I quietly slipped away, I assume the jealous husband looked for me in vain around midnight after my last recorded break. He didn't call me again. I also assumed he was high on drugs or alcohol at the time he called me. Nevertheless, I was extremely happy to have the use of voice track technology. It just may have saved us both a lot of grief.

And, by the way, R.I.P. Lee 'Baby' Simms. He passed away in 2015.

+++

One of the coolest perks of my career had to do with dining. Jan Basham was a promoter for A&M Records in Los

Angeles. She knew how to treat the folks who had anything to do with the artists she represented: Gino Vannelli, the Captain and Tennille, Herb Alpert, Sergio Mendes, Peter Frampton, and many others.

Jan's favorite Hollywood Restaurant to wine and dine disc jockeys, music directors, programmers, promoters, musicians and recording artists—the movers and shakers of L.A. radio, was *Le St. Germain Restaurant* on Melrose Avenue in L.A., where the 'house white' was Kendall-Jackson and the menu non-existent. The L.A. Times put it this way shortly before the world-renowned eatery closed its doors for good in the fall of 1988:

> *"Le St. Germain wraps itself around you as you walk in the door, enclosing you in the sort of luxurious intimacy you just don't find much anymore. As you walk through these dimly lit,*

> *rose-colored rooms and sink into your seat, the outside world disappears. This is an old-fashioned restaurant that caters to your every whim, doing its best to convince you that you are being served in a private home. You never even see a menu; the maitre d' simply comes over and tells you about the sauteed foie gras... the feuilletage of asparagus and crayfish tails... the roast lobster with noodles." (Reichl 1988)*

Of course, most deejays went for the free lunch and especially the free-flowing wine. And so, it wasn't long before I found myself thinking more about the wine than the actual opportunity to schmooze with well-known recording artists. That should have been a tip off that my priorities could cause problems someday. Especially for someone who claimed to be a good, church-going Bible study leader and deacon. 'Lucky' for me the world of Hollywood never intersected with the people I knew and loved at church. So, I could just roll right along in my chameleon suit as happy as a clam.

I was on a disastrous vector... like a plane flown by a blindfolded pilot, headed for Chicago's O'Hare, one of the busiest airports in the world.

+++

Little did I know my days at KPOL (which had just gotten new call letters KZLA) were numbered. Following a year and a half of working at a great radio station with the best people, a new program director was hired with instructions to cut back on the staff. I think he just wanted to make room for one of his friends at the job. Let's face it, I had a choice gig in L.A. And I was the most recent hire. ☹ He gave me an interesting choice, "I can fire the afternoon host, or I can fire you. You choose."

Wow. That was a clever way to let someone go and not take responsibility. He was probably betting that I wasn't going to throw my colleague under the bus. He was right.

Thankfully, I had a job offer in my hip pocket. The same outfit who had run The Loop in Chicago were now running KZOK, a rock station in Seattle.

They offered me a midday position. Kay and I packed our belongings into a moving van (again) and headed way up north on Interstate 5 to the Emerald City. We found a great little house in West Seattle to rent and moved in.

Easy come. Easy go. We were in Seattle for only three months. Selfishly and unbelievably, I resigned after such a short time. I really missed L.A. (cue the world's smallest violin, poor baby) and the ocean, the sunshine—especially the sunshine, which was at a premium in Seattle. It was December, the rainiest and gloomiest time of the year. I fell victim to S.A.D. – Seasonal Affective Disorder. The amount of cloud cover and rain in December was voluminous, so we left.

One of my biggest contributors to having 'one foot in the world and one foot in the church' was (some might argue IS) selfishness or self-centeredness. And of course, my old friend Pride who often crashed the party uninvited while rearing its ugly head.

I was offered a morning position at KFOX in sunny Redondo Beach and so… we hit Interstate 5 AGAIN, this time headed south.

On the way, I had a gallbladder attack and was admitted to the ER in Los Banos—a community aptly named. *Los Banos* is, quite literally, 'The Bathrooms' in Spanish. Seriously? Who would name their town that? "So, Mr. Noble, where do you live?"

"Well, me and the family live in "The Bathrooms."

"Really? Isn't that a bit crowded?"

"Oh no, and besides, we're not much on clean air. It's all a hoax you know." In all fairness, *Los Banos* was named after a local creek, but still, the word 'desolate' comes to mind. That part of the San Joaquin Valley is bereft of trees and cool weather. It was February 1980, and it was hot.

The station paid for the bulk of the move but moving is still expensive and hard on one's marriage too.

After a single year at KFOX, I was let go because the new general manager and I did not hit it off. He wanted to take the station in a different direction. I didn't want to go there; so, he fired me. I applied for a part time job at K-WEST—a legendary rock station in L.A. They gave me a lot of fill-in work and I had a weekend shift as well. But the best part of working at K-WEST was working with J.J. Jackson and my rock jock hero, China Smith!

China Smith inspired me with his smooth on-air, hip persona. He just sounded cool. And he had a rich, deep voice. Most importantly, he always sounded like he was having a good time—that he enjoyed what he was doing. So, it was just awesome to fill-in for China Smith. China passed, much too early, in 2005 from a heart attack. He was fifty-six.

In 1981, not long after K-WEST Program Director Ted Ferguson hired me, the station flipped format and was going to let everyone go. I had a chance to chat with one of the jocks, J.J. Jackson, about the flip. When I asked JJ what he was going to do, he said, "I've got this gig with a new outfit in New York City. It's called MTV. I'm moving to the 'Big Apple' to become a VIDEO jock!"

And that's exactly what he did. J.J. was one of the five original VJs on MTV. He died in 2004.

+++

I was beginning to become a familiar face at the Post Office—once more sending out tapes of my show and resumes to a dozen or so prospects. (It can get expensive sending out packages that cost roughly $5 a pop.) This time I got a great offer with Greater Media's K-HITS Los Angeles. The best part? We didn't have to move!!

They were best known for their morning host, the legendary Charlie Tuna. He obviously chose that name; I don't think a parent would name their child Charlie Tuna. But it was a memorable radio name.

That's him, standing, center.

K-HITS kept me busy. They hired me for middays 10am-2pm. So, every weekday I followed Charlie Tuna on the air. Those were wonderful days where I learned so much watching the 'Tuna Man' as I called him. Charlie was a pro's pro. And my family life was finally stable for more than four years.

Naturally, this being a media outfit, there were some attractive people in the front office. Listeners and visitors just expected that. It wasn't long before I sometimes found myself flirting with a couple of them. It's like the seductive commercial from one of the current online dating services, "It doesn't hurt to look."

Well, in truth, it does. Because if you like what you see, the next thing you know, you're telling yourself, "Well, it doesn't hurt to touch." Don't go there because doing so can erode whatever relationship you may already have. Again, I was married to a beautiful, young, and awesome woman. Why on God's green earth would I ever be interested in 'greener pastures'... which they never were by the way. No, I didn't 'touch', but the fact that I flirted spoke volumes about my pride.

+++

CHAPTER 10

FASTEN YOUR SEATBELTS

The truth is, I didn't really like this kind of gig. I mean, everybody looked at the emcee and I stood out like a pimple on your nose!

As I mentioned earlier, even though I had left the Academy, I still wanted to fly. And when I finally got my pilot's license in the 80s, I was so excited. Originally, I had thought this would be a dream I could only fulfill through enrollment with the Air Force, but here I was a pilot!

Prior to getting my license in 1981, I had to complete a couple cross country solo flights out of Santa Monica Airport. It's a few miles north of LAX, and while it's not as busy, it's busy enough for a new pilot.

My first cross country took me north over the LA metro and across the San Fernando Valley, one more mountain range and then it was clear 'sailing' all the way to Lompoc—a small coastal community near Santa Barbara in Central California. Here it was, my moment of truth, I was to file a flight plan, fly there, gas up and return...all alone. Piece of cake, right? Not exactly.

Although I was a bit nervous, I knew I could handle the trip, after all, this was what I had trained for.

The plane was quick to put my ego in check at takeoff. Since I was the only one in the aircraft, it climbed a lot faster than it had during training when there was another person on board to weigh the plane down. No worries at all. I took a deep breath and continued my way. Now that I was in the air, it was sure to be smooth sailing as I headed northwest. Except... I forgot to turn my transponder on, 'D'oh!'.

This was my first solo rookie mistake. Every pilot knows, turning on the transponder is very important because if you don't have it on, chances are the ATC (Air Traffic Control) radar won't see you.

After taking off and crossing the Santa Monica Mountains, to my immediate east was Burbank Airport; another very busy airport. As I crossed the mountains (about 3,000' in altitude) and entered the San Fernando Valley, I saw a DC9 that had just taken off and was rising quickly from my right and perpendicular to my course. My skills were about to be put to the test. I knew when he passed over me there was a good chance, I'd be flying through his wake turbulence— aka wingtip vortices. All I could do was hold my breath. If I had remembered to turn my transponder on, air traffic control would have redirected me. It was a scary moment, but one that taught me a very valuable lesson. If ATC can't see you, it's possible other pilots, in one of the most crowded air spaces in the world, can't see you either. Turns out I missed the wake turbulence by a mile. Whew!

On my second cross country, I had to go over the San Gabriel mountains flying east and then north over them. The San Gabriel mountains are the same mountains you'd see in the background of an L.A. skyline picture postcard on a clear day. Great for pictures, not so much for flying. They rise roughly 10,000 feet above the Los Angeles Basin.

When the marine layer comes in from the coast and hits the mountain range it goes straight up the side of the mountain. This is called a "mountain wave" and I had very little training with it. I was expecting to go up a little bit, but it was like all of a sudden, a giant grabbed my plane and shot me straight up at a climb rate of 2000 feet per minute, which is really fast, especially in a Cessna 172. I pushed down on the yoke (steering column or steering wheel) firmly to slow the 172 down and to keep it from entering a stall attitude as it raced upward.

It's like a roller coaster. The wave of fast-moving air takes you straight up and then... well, as soon as it leveled out high above the mountain, I said "uh oh." At which point, the 'wave' pulled the yoke violently and the 172 lurched forward, then down. I could barely keep control as I descended faster than I had risen. I pulled back so hard on the yoke I thought the wings were going to come off! Thankfully, I leveled out around 3,000 feet above the ground. On the way back, instead of going over the mountain, I decided to fly through the canyon about 500 feet above the highway. There was no way I was going to fly over the top of the San Gabriel mountains of roller coaster terror again until I had more training.

+++

As a working member of the media in a great job, a great air shift that offered tremendous visibility, I was frequently offered the chance to do some very interesting (if not potentially dangerous) promotions. Remember, I had already survived a hot air balloon crash ten years earlier. No matter. I picked myself up and was ready to ride that horse again!

One of the truly most fun times I had in radio was flying for four hours over the L.A. metro with the Miller Squadron—six WWII era SNJ-2s that flew in formation and 'sky-typed' dot-matrix messages across L.A.'s epic blue skies using dots and dashes of white smoke that each plane was equipped to discharge in a computerized and synched sequence.

They were known as the "Sky-typers." I was given a parachute (a kiss for good luck, LOL) and a backseat in one of the SNJ-2 aircraft—a single-engine propeller-driven Navy trainer with a sliding bubble canopy.

Their 'typing' looked really cool in the sky and would last a couple of minutes before the high-altitude winds took care of it. The sky-typing was typically done at ten-thousand feet because of all the local air traffic at lower altitudes, especially in, near and around LAX.

The pilots were all well-experienced and had flown in combat during the Korean War, meaning at least a few of them were getting a little 'long in the tooth.' But these gray hairs knew how to fly and have fun and get the job done. My pilot even did a 360-degree barrel roll when we were done with our messages recalling a similar personality trait and maneuver in a T-33 jet some 15 years earlier while I was at the Air Force Academy. He was a showoff. They were both showoffs, and I loved it! (In whisper voice: "I think they did too!" ☺)

Another time, I was invited, along with our oldest daughter who was about 8 years old at the time, for a ride on board the Goodyear Blimp Columbia! And because I had a pilot's license, the pilot changed seats with me so I could fly the blimp… AND I DID!! What fun!!! I logged thirty minutes PIC (pilot in command) flying the Goodyear Blimp. By the way, max speed is about 35mph. I didn't worry about other aircraft because we were so large in the sky that nobody could miss seeing us.

In the early 80s my program director asked if I'd like to call in reports from a helicopter that would be hovering over the RMS Queen Mary for a Beach Boys anniversary concert in

Long Beach, permanent home of the QM. That was fun, but kinda scary too.

As you may know, many 'choppers' don't have doors, so I made sure my seat belt was SECURE! While we did fly around a bit, we mostly hovered at a higher altitude than we would have otherwise flown—two thousand feet above the Queen Mary so my radio call-ins could have clear line-of-sight to the hill where the radio receiver antenna was located. Hovering for a half hour or so at a time felt a bit sketchy... kinda queasy to me. Like what was holding us up??? Oh, must be that big nut and washer on top of the blades holding them down. In the military, they call that the 'Jesus nut' because if it breaks or comes off, the next thing that happens is an impromptu 'meeting' with Jesus.

In the early 90s and while working at KJQY San Diego, I was privileged to fly right seat on a Beechcraft Starship. The avionics were state of the art and the plane featured a 'canard' design. Which meant there were small wings near the nose of the craft and the propellers were backwards, pushing the aircraft. It was a blast!!

And while at K-LOVE, I was offered a once-in-a-lifetime chance to fly around Denver in a vintage B-17 bomber. I wore my dad's WWII medals for the ride to honor his service. It was fantastic! The pilots invited me to crawl under their feet to the all-plexiglass, nose ball-turret which housed a 50 cal machine gun. As I imagined taking aim at Messerschmitt 109s, it was sobering to realize all but my backside was exposed to 'enemy gunfire' in that bubble turret.

All of these 'in air' radio promotions were right up my alley and I truly consider myself blessed to have them on my list of amazing life experiences.

+++

As a pilot, I suppose I could say that life is all about the take-off and the landing. You may have heard the saying, "Flying is hours of boredom punctuated by a few seconds of sheer terror." Crosswinds can make any landing... how shall we put it... dicey. A crosswind landing takes a fair amount of skill and experience—two commodities I had in short supply. A cross wind occurs when the wind isn't coming from directly in front of the plane and the pilot needs to head towards the runway left or right of center. In other words, the plane may be headed toward the runway, however, it is 'crabbing' at a slight angle into the wind. The stronger the wind, the greater the angle and more power is required. The same thing happens in your boat when the current in a river, for example, keeps you from pointing directly toward the shore or the dock.

If we apply this principle to our faith, we learn that God set out a lot of boundaries in the Bible, things which are meant to keep us on a straight path. Sometimes we go with the flow, and sometimes we encounter moral crosswinds and tend to get a little off kilter... even crooked.

It was the mid-80s; we were living in San Clemente, and I was on the midday shift at K-HITS in L.A., whenever I had some extra time and money, I would make my way over to Orange County Airport and pick up a couple lessons. Since you're not allowed to fly solo unless you've made three takeoffs and landings within the past ninety days, I was typically with an instructor. This day, I was ok with that.

> *"Twenty-six miles across the sea*
> *Santa Catalina is a waitin' for me.*
> *Santa Catalina, the island of romance,*
> *romance, romance, romance."* —The Four Preps, 1957

Santa Catalina Island was visible from our condo in San Clemente whenever the skies were clear. It was a beautiful site to see from a distance. But we were about to get an up-close view of the island. With the instructor, my wife, her friend Rhonda, and myself we were at max capacity for the Cessna 172. I had flown to Catalina before, so I knew about the flaw in its runway—a sort of rise in the middle of the runway which causes half the runway to appear to DISappear as you flare the plane for landing. The runway is at the very top of the island some 1600 feet above sea level and is surrounded by steep, rocky cliffs on all sides including the approach and take off points. Basically, it's like landing on a ginormous aircraft carrier.

In early 1984, there was a terrible accident involving a private jet that crashed for this very reason. Upon flaring just before touching down, the pilot, who had never flown into this airport, experienced the illusion that half the runway vanishes and decided to lift back off, but he hesitated, and by the time he re-engaged the throttle, he wasn't going fast enough. The aircraft went over the cliff at the end of the runway killing six people. Terrible thing because ultimately the runway was too short for the Learjet in the first place. That 'small' detail should have been caught in pre-flight.

I knew I needed to approach the island kind of high but when I did the plane got caught in a gust of wind which turned us at a slightly different angle. I made the mistake of saying, "Oops."

If you're the one operating the vehicle which everyone is riding in, no one wants to hear you utter that word. The instructor was calm, probably because he knew he had the ability to take over if we were in real danger, but Kay and Rhonda… not so much.

We were crabbing. When this happens, if the plane is not straightened out at the last moment, a tire could be blown, the landing gear could be damaged, you might cause the aircraft to do a ground roll (not good) or worst-case scenario, at this airport, you could slide off the edge of the island (also not good). I got the plane straightened out just before we touched down, no damage to the plane. Only to my pride.

I suppose I could have added that to the title, *Culture Jock: Just Crabbing Along*. But I imagine I'd probably be approached at book signings with, "You're nothing like I expected."

+++

Halloween 1984, K-HITS sponsored a costume contest at a local bar and grill giving me another opportunity to imbibe, but I had to be careful because I was the emcee and host.

It didn't stop me completely, which should have been eye-opening about my growing addiction. In addition, Kay was now hip to my sneakiness. Yes, I was becoming sneakier all the time, what else would you call downing an entire beer in the car within about ten seconds? Did you see 'Flight' with Denzel? Same thing only without the cocaine.

You'd think it would have occurred to me that she who can smell alcohol breath in the next county would know that I had sucked down a beer, or two, before walking into the house. But no. I needed the buzz. She knew and quietly (sometimes not so quietly) let me know she did not like it!!! We were beginning to move in different directions.

So, back to the K-HITS costume contest. Already boisterous folks were emboldened because nobody knew who they were, hiding behind their party masks. They became SUPER boisterous when beer and wine were added to the mix. Yes, it was loud. Very loud. So loud I could barely hear.

I had on a white suit with white shirt and tie and looked pretty spiffy, if I do say so myself. The truth is, I didn't really like this kind of gig. I mean, everybody looked at the emcee and I stood out like a pimple on your nose! Besides, I'm an introvert by nature. My job forced me to learn how to be extroverted, but I was never comfortable with it. In fact, I would volunteer to lead singing at church to gain experience appearing in front of people. We worshiped at a small community church... about fifty in average attendance, so it wasn't intimidating at all.

It was almost time to announce the winners of the contest!

There were several finalists in the lineup. I recall Cinderella and Dracula were the runners-up... and then... and then... (wait for it) the big moment when the night's best costume winner would be announced. One of the staff whispered to me, "The 'morphodite' won." At least, 'morphodite' is what I heard. What she was saying was 'hermaphrodite'... but thanks to all the noise, all I heard was morphodite.

"Ladies and gentlemen, let's have a big hand for the Morphodite."

Somebody close to me said, "Did he just say 'morphodite'?"

"Nah. Nobody would say that."

It was so noisy I got away with coining what I thought was a new word. But I felt really stupid. Oh well, they'll just say, "He's just a deejay and deserves our love and forgiveness." Of course, if you believe that, you'll believe that Dracula always donated blood for good causes… just not his own! (bada-BING! bada-BOOM!)

The word 'morphodite' is actually a real word—an abbreviated form of 'hermaphrodite' and started showing up in the English language a couple of centuries ago. Nowadays, nobody uses it. Except me of course, haha!

> *"Humor is not a mood, but a way of looking at the world."*
> —Ludwig Wittgenstein

Humor has always been interwoven into my daily existence. Even in instances where I become the punchline, such as the Halloween party. But I think everyone can agree, there is nothing funnier than the things our children say. Especially when they are said in a state of complete innocence.

In 1995, I was working at KACD Santa Monica, California. Our home was in Irvine. Our first son, Kenny, Jr. was 5 years old and going to kindergarten. One day, I was walking him home from his kindergarten – only a couple hundred yards away from our rented condo and we passed a young couple embracing each other on a blanket as they were both napping on this beautiful, sunny SoCal day. Kenny looked up at me after staring at them, "Are they okay?"

I chuckled, "Yes, they just like each other a lot."
Kenny said, "Oh that's good. I thought they were dead."
Another day, Kay was putting together a shopping list and we were all at the kitchen table. She glanced over the list once more then said, "We need bread, hamburger meat, chips and laundry detergent. What else do we need?" At that moment, Kenny, Jr. who had been quietly playing with his Legos spoke up and said quite seriously, "Well, we're all out of balloons."

We all had a good laugh, even Kenny although he didn't understand why we all thought what he said was so funny. With so many things which can form a punchline or be found humorous it almost seems people must go out of their way to be sour or grumpy. Or maybe I still have some growing up to do... I suppose it could swing either way. Singer, actor, and entertainer Maurice Chevalier once said, *"You don't stop laughing because you grow older. You grow older because you stop laughing."*

If that's the case, maybe it has been the punchlines which have gotten me this far.

+++

CHAPTER 11

L.A. PART TWO— DISASTER

When he didn't report after taking off, none of us knew what was going on... until it was reported that his plane had crashed and there were no survivors.

In 1985, after four great years, I decided to leave KHTZ for a union job across the street at KFI/KOST. KFI was the AM station and KOST was the FM. I was excited because KOST was the number one contemporary station in Los Angeles and I would be reunited with my first real friend in L.A., Mike Sakellarides. You may recall Mike was the afternoon host at KZLA FM seven years earlier (1978). We still keep in touch today and remind each other of how fortunate we were to find such good life partners. He and Barbara are two of the nicest people I know. And I could never have found a woman as good as Kay. She is IT for me.

So, why didn't I put HER first instead of my career?

Because I defined who I was by *what I did*. Not who I *did things for*. As a Christian I should have known that I had it backwards. As such, I focused on being the best that I could be at the exclusion of my wife and family so that I could make more money to buy bigger and better things. That's a perfect formula for drifting apart.

And we did.

+++

If you have never had an addiction, then you can't really relate to any of my struggles and you are blessed with more contentment than most.

My addiction has been like the Hydra of Lerma. The Hydra is a mythical serpentine water monster from Greek mythology. Picture a dragon with no wings and an extra-long snake-like head. When you're trying to kill a snake, you simply cut off the head, right? Well, unlike a regular snake, if you cut off the head of a hydra, it was said that two more would grow back in its place. Just when you think it's dead and no longer a problem it comes back to rear its ugly head but this time with reinforcements.

If you have ever seen the animated movie *Hercules*, there is a scene where Hercules attacks the hydra. He goes to fight this beast with pride. He wants everyone to know he is a hero. He swings his sword like a maniac chopping off one head after another which causes more and more and more heads for him to deal with. At some point, his trainer says, "Enough with the heads!"

That's about how my life as a Christian has gone. I go at things with pride, trying to make things happen on my own and Jesus is off to the side saying, "Kenny, it's not working. Are you ready to try things my way?"

You may ask how I can live with myself after all these failures? First, this book condenses the time between my 'failures' and they seem to add up quickly. But remember, all these things happened over a 43-year career. Secondly and most importantly, I can live with myself because of Grace. I don't sin so that 'grace may yet abound', I sin because I'm human. I know that the Potter knows this and continues to shape me as he wants me because he loves me. His death on the cross has given me value. If I have breath in me, I can grow according to his will.

I referred to this earlier, but this verse written by Paul bears repeating: *"Nothing good lives in me, that is, in my sinful nature. I want to do what is right, but I can't. I want to do what is good but I don't. I don't want to do what is wrong, but I do it anyway."* (Romans 7:18) Paul's agony contained in this letter to the Romans translates as hope for those of us who are caught up in addictions – alcohol, drugs, lust, food, nicotine, etc. – and we are inclined to beat ourselves up… over and over and over. Like Paul, *"I love God's law with all my heart, but there is another power within me that is at war with my mind. This power makes me a slave to the sin that is still within me… the answer is in Jesus Christ our Lord!"* (Romans 7:22-25)

And so, I pray: "Amen and THANK YOU FATHER! Please do not let the Enemy steal my joy in the salvation you have freely given me and anyone else who wants it. Help me realize greater things can be accomplished when I stop swinging and instead submit fully to you and your ways."

+++

It was at KFI/KOST that I qualified for my SAG (Screen Actors Guild) card, which has since morphed into a SAG/AFTRA (American Federation of Television and Radio Artists) card. I receive a small pension and as a member in good standing, am privileged to vote for the annual SAG awards show. And to ensure I make an informed vote; SAG sends me DVDs of all the best movies from the year. Sadly (in my opinion) most of them are rated 'R' and are difficult to watch. It is especially disturbing that the use of the 'F' word has become so commonplace. For me, there is no place for films that demonstrate that level of egregiousness. Like it or not, they are shaping culture and, in most cases, not for the better.

I was hired at union scale – $61K a year and that was pretty darn good in 1985. When I arrived, the great comedy duo of Lohman and Barkley were hosting mornings on KFI. But the long-running show was in trouble. Roger Barkley surprisingly walked out and when he resigned, Gary Owens stepped in to fill the vacuum that Barkley created. Owens was teamed with Al Lohman giving the show a bit of a 'Laugh In' hue in morning drive. They were hilarious.

Gary Owens was the <u>hand-on-the-ear-announcer-in-the-booth</u> on *Rowan and Martin's 'Laugh In'* during the late 60s.

It was my job to go into the main studio and replace tapes of commercials with current content. And that's when I could do a limited visit. Maybe only for a few seconds because they were so busy, but I definitely got to know the guys.

Gary Owens always wore a suit. His hair was always perfect, and he wore glasses. I never wore suits on the air—always t-shirts and jeans. And… I'm no Gary Owens, LOL ☺

+++

KOST played a lot of sentimental, soft love songs. It was Program Director Jhani Kaye who created the program *Love Songs on the KOST*. From 1985 to late '86, I was the producer and slaved away over a hot Ampex 2-inch tape deck – recording, mixing, leveling, mastering, and indeed sweating over all the early episodes of Love Songs, which reached its zenith under the gifted Ted Ziegenbusch and Liz Kiley in the mid-to-late 80s.

They read a lot of mushy letters—the ones that could draw out emotion in listeners who could relate to losing a love of their lives, or surprising that special someone with a ring or a situation that involved a terminal disease where the patient would request a love song for a special boy or girl friend. And of course, the song would be a two-hanky tearjerker, guaranteed to bring you back the next evening for another episode of *Love Songs on the KOST*. I filled in for the Love

Songs hosts every now and then. It's a demanding show and more challenging and stressful than hosting morning drive!

+++

Thanks to my brother Lawrence, a Civil War reenactor, we both had an opportunity to play as extras in the ABC TV mini-series *North and South, Book* 2 produced at Walt Disney's Golden Oak Ranch in Newhall, California. Most folks just called it the Disney Ranch. That's where they filmed Bonanza, Back to The Future, and a gazillion westerns, movies and TV series.

My brother asked if I wanted to be a part of it. I asked my Program Director, Jhani Kaye, if I could adjust my hours at work so that I could be on the set at 5am. He agreed!! All I would have to do was record interviews with the director and the stars, which I did. Thanks to Jhani, I was able to interview Mary Crosby, Parker Stevenson, Whip Hubley and director Kevin Connor. Portions of those interviews aired on KFI Los Angeles.

Lawrence and I were extras and played both Yankees and Rebels. We were in every episode. It was so much fun. It was like we were kids again.

I even got a full-on close-up, and you could see my face behind my rifle taking up the whole screen. The director said, "Act like you fired it and we'll do the rest."

My big scene did NOT end up on the cutting room floor. It was indeed in the mini-series! Smoke and fire appeared right out of the rifle on the episode that aired my scene. It looked exactly as if I fired the weapon. I was impressed with the postproduction of that scene.

All of this was well and good, and worked out nicely, but I still wanted to be a full-time deejay.

+++

There was also great sadness at KFI/KOST. Kay and I were especially saddened on our 15th wedding anniversary, June 4, 1986. That's when veteran traffic reporter Bruce Wayne was killed just after takeoff in his Cessna Cardinal from Fullerton Airport. It was around 6am and I had just arrived for work. When he didn't report after taking off about 6:15, none of us knew what was going on… until it was reported that his plane had crashed and there were no survivors. Wayne, like myself, was a candidate for the Journalist in Space program, which had become another 'casualty' of the Challenger explosion on January 28th. We both had aspirations to fly in space. Wayne left this Earth, but sadly, not the way he had intended. He was a great pilot, traffic reporter, colleague, and friend.

But before the end of the day, lightning would strike for a second time. KFI/KOST General Manager Don Dalton had been in Miami for meetings when he got the word about Wayne's death. He immediately got on a flight and came back to Los Angeles as fast as he could. As he walked across the KFI parking lot, Dalton dropped from what appeared to be a brain aneurysm. He died the next day.

May they both rest in peace.

Life can get rugged at times, and it often seems that the ruggedness happens when we least expect it. That's why it's so important to appreciate your friends, loved ones and family because none of us ever knows. I, along with the entire staff at KFI/KOST went home that day shell-shocked, and I made sure to give Kay and the girls extra hugs and kisses when I got home.

+++

MEMO

TO: KLSX, KRLA STAFF   DATE: 10/24/86
FROM: DON HAGEN
RE: BILLY JUGGS, KENNY NOBLE

I'M PLEASED TO ANNOUNCE THAT BILLY JUGGS AND KENNY NOBLE WILL MOVE TO THEIR PERMANENMT ON-AIR POSITIONS AT KLSX ON MONDAY, OCTOBER 27TH.

ALTHOUGH BILLY HAS BEEN HELPING US ON MORNING DRIVE FOR THE PAST TWO WEEKS, HE WILL BE HEARD REGULARLY ON KLSX FROM 6 TO 10 IN THE EVENING, MONDAY THROUGH FRIDAY. AS MANY OF YOU KNOW, BILLY COMES TO US DIRECTLY FROM KMET, AND IS AN INTEGRAL PART OF THE ALBUM ROCK RADIO COMMUNITY HERE IN LOS ANGELES.

RETURNING TO US FROM KFI/KOST IS KENNY NOBLE, THE NEW MORNING DRIVE MAN ON KLSX, 6 TO 10 WEEKDAY MORNINGS. KENNY BRINGS WITH HIM A GREAT ON-AIR STYLE AND EXTENSIVE KNOWLEDGE OF ALBUM ROCK FROM STATIONS HERE (KWST), CHICAGO (WLUP), HOUSTON (KLOL), AND SEATTLE (KZOK).

WE ARE VERY FORTUNATE TO HAVE EXCELLENT COMMUNICATORS LIKE BILLY AND KENNY ON OUR TEAM. I'M LOOKING FORWARD TO WORKING WITH EACH OF THEM AND I HOPE YOU'LL JOIN ME IN WELCOMING THEM TO KLSX.

THANKS.

PS: ALSO ON MONDAY: RICK DIEGO MOVES TO 10PM TO 2AM,
    DANA LAUREN TO THE 10AM TO 2PM SLOT
    AND GUY DAVIS MOVES TO 2PM TO 6PM.

CHAPTER 12

WHEN PUSH COMES TO SHOVE

In a haunting echo of the words I had heard before, he said, "So Ken, what can I do for you." The last time he said that to me I exploded in hate.

After a year and a half, I left KOST for my dream job—the first full-time morning host on KLSX Classic Rock for Southern California. HALLELUJAH!!! KLSX was classic rock, AND they were right across the street. It was 1986 and one of the first classic rock stations in the country. They were upgrading from tape cartridges to CDs. And finally, I was back in the saddle as a disc jockey!

The job only offered $48K but consultant Don Hagen told me I could match my previous salary with bonuses. I took the pay cut and transferred to KLSX. I should have consulted with Kay about this 'opportunity' to take a lower salary, but I made the decision unilaterally. (And I wondered why she thought I was controlling. Ugh!) Bringing her in just might have saved us from separating because I only worked there for four months. The job began in late October 1986, and I would be working with one of L.A.'s most recognizable and beautiful women—Joni Caryl. Which would also prove to be a serious temptation to deal with. Playboy magazine came to town and decided to do an expose of the female deejays in L.A.

I promised myself I would not look at any of the revealing photos of my co-host. I kept my promise so I could look my wife in the eye and tell her honestly that I had not seen those pictures. *'Cha-ching.'* That was the sound of a major deposit in our love bank. But, unknown to me, I was already overdrawn, and our marriage was holding on by a thread. Making a point not to look at the photos was too little too late. Instead of putting so much emphasis on what I *shouldn't* be doing I could have added value to both our lives by focusing more on the things I *should* have been doing. Giving time and attention to Kay and the girls.

The worst year of my life— 1987, was going to unfold in dramatic fashion.

In February, I got news from my mom that dad had terminal lung cancer. I flew out to Tampa on Tuesday and came back on Saturday. While I was gone KLSX management decided to let me go. And the reason was because rock giant KMET, the Mighty Met—a major competitor—let some of their well known, heritage deejays go after flipping to a new format. KLSX picked up a couple of those well-known deejays who were on the street. Kay didn't have to say it. I knew it. I owned this difficult turn of events.

I learned an important lesson. I had prayed my brains out that God would give me this job. I thought it would solve all my problems and I 'begged, borrowed and stole' to get the job. So, God answered my prayer swiftly and gave me the job on a silver platter... only to have it ripped away four months later. The lesson? Be careful what you pray for because sometimes it's not in your best interest to have whatever it is you're praying for. I had not sought wisdom. I simply wanted the job. Kenny Noble Cortes always seems to learn the hard way.

A year and a half earlier, I was chosen to be the voiceover host for the nationally syndicated TV show, *Top 40 videos*. All I had to do was read the scripts and get paid 300 bucks a week. By February of 1987, following my return from Florida, I was fired from that job as well. They said it was because of sagging revenues. That made sense. MTV was on the rise and *Top 40 Videos* was a syndicated show that was on a different channel in every market. They just couldn't compete with the technological advances in cable TV broadcasting and the huge reach of MTV. And look at me, trying to compete with one of my jock heroes, J.J. Jackson! *Top 40 Videos* fell on hard times and eventually ceased production altogether.

While my underlying problems really began with me and my obsession for getting ahead and putting career first, family second, and Kay last, the Enemy, always one to kick you when you're down, introduced a new actor—Pastor Jimmy.

CULTURE JOCK

November 1986 is when our church in San Clemente got a new pastor. This pastor came from Ohio. Pastor Jimmy was an all-right guy (on the surface anyway) and I helped him, his wife and two kids move in. Kay was the church secretary, and it wasn't long before they developed a close relationship, unknown to me.

Kay and I hosted a weekly bible study in our home. This was April 1987. I said I had to go to bed around eight. I was rather fond of saying something like, "Hey, if I drop dead right now, I'll get five and a half hours of sleep." That's because I had to get up at 0-dark hundred to be at my new morning job at KyXy in San Diego by 5am.

Everybody pretty much started leaving after that. Everybody that is, except one person. So, that was about 8:30 at night. I woke up around 11pm to the sound of people talking. Pastor Jimmy and Kay were in the living room chatting and thoroughly enjoying their conversation. I was annoyed and said, "Jimmy, it's kind of late, don't you think? Shouldn't you be home with your family?"

I could tell he was interested in Kay, and I was bothered by that.

When June rolled around, Kay called a meeting with me and the elders of our church at our house where she announced that she no longer loved me and wanted a separation. She did not mention Pastor Jimmy because she didn't want him to lose his job and wanted this whole situation to look good to the church. But I knew it was because of Jimmy. I assumed he and my wife had planned this out to give himself time to get another job and then Kay would divorce me, Jimmy would divorce his wife, and Kay would be his.

There really was no way to put a positive spin on what happened. She was leaving me, period. And that was the worst thing that had ever happened to me.

You could have knocked me over with a feather. I think at times like this, people (generally men) who define who they are by their jobs, tend to say things like, "I didn't have a clue." or "I didn't see this coming." Well, in retrospect, had I given my situation ANY thought, the signs were everywhere that our marriage was in trouble. Kay had become distant. And like the lyrics from the Sanford-Townsend Band song, there seemed to be 'Smoke from a Distant Fire' in her eyes. If only I'd known.

I *should* have known. Had I taken the time, I would have.

We had been married for sixteen years at this point and our marriage should have been rock solid. But because I wasn't there to listen… rather I was there to work on the next day's show, it was pretty much sealed in cement that we were headed for a train wreck. Instead of prepping for a great show I was prepping for a failed marriage.

Thankfully (for my state of mind), Kay wanted to do this 'right', so she and our daughters left the house to spend the next three months with good friends of ours who also attended the same church. The girls were twelve and nine at the time.

I was left at the house by myself. I also began worshipping at a different church so Kay and the girls could continue to worship at our church in San Clemente.

I spent day and night on my knees crying and begging for a miracle. The few notes I tried to send to Kay were ignored. I started a diary which helped a little bit.

And then I got angry. Really angry. I knew in my heart that Pastor Jimmy had emotionally seduced my wife. A week had gone by and without thinking of the consequences, I marched down to the church office a short distance away. Kay was at the front desk and saw me approaching as I'm sure Pastor Jimmy did too. She said, "Ken… what's going on?"

I yelled at the top of my voice that I had something to say to Pastor Jimmy. And by the way, the church office was in a multi-office suite and there were people nearby working at other jobs. They became silent and watched like they were witnesses to a mugging. And they were… a drive-by verbal mugging!

At that moment, Pastor Jimmy came out of his office and said in measured tones, "Ken. What can I do for you?"

I glared at him intensely and shouted, "I hate you for what you've done to my marriage, and I hate your G.. d… church!" I was shocked at the words that came out of my mouth, but I was so angry. He was taken aback by my offensive language. He looked like I had a gun and was going to shoot him. If I'd had a gun, I might have. That's how angry I was. Instead, I turned and marched back home where I fell on the floor in tears and begged God's forgiveness for my words against Him.

My new job at KyXy in San Diego didn't help any. All we did was play saccharine love songs that tormented me. I had never listened to the words but now I was intensely listening, and it seemed every song was about me and Kay. I would literally be in tears in the control room where I was almost always alone—just me and my microphone. At the conclusion of any song, I would have a few seconds to throw on a smile and do my announcements.

I was a basket case.

That was a full-time job, and I also got a part time job doing weekends in L.A. So, I was working seven days a week and didn't have much time to feel sorry for myself except when I was at the radio station playing syrupy love songs that had suddenly become intensely personal.

Talk about a candid look behind the 'velvet ropes'!

Weekends, I deejayed for an easy listening satellite radio network with about 300 affiliates. We distributed our various radio formats including the 'Joy' network from the Sunset/Vine Tower in Hollywood. If I hadn't been such a bundle of nerves, I would have enjoyed this very cool place to work a lot more. Speaking of nerves, I also came down with shingles during this time and here I had just turned forty. Could it get any worse?

Before the Enemy could hit me with another catastrophe, God had mercy on me and gave me my miracle.

+++

On a Thursday in mid-August—three months after the separation began, and around lunchtime, the elders from Kay's church called me and asked to meet at 2pm. I said "Sure!" San Clemente is approximately midway between L.A. and San Diego. Took me less than an hour to get home.

I didn't have a clue as to why they wanted to talk. I thought they were finally getting around to my outburst at the church office. I went to the meeting preparing for this and hoping they might show just a little mercy. Turns out I didn't need any at that moment.

The elders requested that I sit down and listen. They told me they received a letter from Pastor Jimmy's former church in Ohio regarding two previous churches he had worked at. The first sentence of the letter went like this... I remember it like it was read to me yesterday,

> *"Dear San Clemente Elders,*
> *Beware of Pastor Jimmy, he is a wolf in sheep's clothing...."*

They went on to talk about two marriages that Pastor Jimmy had wrecked at previous churches. It was the same M-O he had snared Kay with. He ruined his own marriage in the process. His wife finally found out what was going on and his feelings for Kay. But the news hit me like lightning.

"That's my miracle!!!" I shouted to myself.

They told me they were going to meet with Kay later in the day and read the letter to her. And that they were going to let Pastor Jimmy go. God was in motion! YES!! I couldn't contain my joy!! God gave me a miracle, but I still had to wait for Kay's response.

Come Saturday morning, I was at my part time job in L.A. and Kay called me on the hotline. This was the first time we had spoken to one another in three months. She said, "I want to give our marriage a second chance."

I was stunned, then elated! I had already promised God multiple times since the elders read the letter to me, that if I could get Kay back, I would take her back 100% unconditionally. I figured if God could unconditionally love me then I could unconditionally love Kay. I thanked God for the San Clemente elders who were all men of character and blessed with the integrity of honest men.

Pastor Jimmy was let go.

But wait. There's more.

Before we continue chronologically, let's fast forward ten years to 1997. I was working as morning host at WFLC Coast 97.3 in Miami. A lot of water had gone under that proverbial bridge. As a result of the miracle of our reconciliation in 1987 Kay and I were blessed with *two sons* born in 1990 and 1993. So, we had two daughters, waited fifteen years, and had two sons. For me, that's about as good as it gets!

But it's not the end of this story, because Pastor Jimmy would make another appearance in a big way.

In our fourth year in SoFla, 2001, we learned that the church had hired an associate pastor from Ohio. Turns out he was Pastor Jimmy's dad! In the words of Bogey from *Casablanca*, "Of all the gin joints in all the towns in all the world, (s)he walks into mine."

Bob and his wife Carol were good people. They had been part of the 'crew' that helped move Pastor Jimmy and his family to San Clemente back in 1986, unloading the truck and helping them get into their new apartment. You get to know people pretty well when everyone is chipping in to make the job of moving more efficient and fun. And having pizza and sodas afterward makes the occasion festive.

On the way home from church, after we had heard about Pastor Jimmy's dad coming to SoFla, Kay said, "You know… it's only a matter of time before Pastor Jimmy shows up to visit his parents."

Mmm. I hadn't thought of that, but fourteen years after he almost mortally wounded our marriage, there was no bitterness or resentment. After all, Kay and I were closer than ever, and we had two sons to celebrate!

Nevertheless, about six months after Pastor Bob was hired, Kay's prophetic words were realized. As we pulled into the church parking lot one Sunday, she exclaimed, "There he is!!"

I said, "Oh boy. Here we go."

I parked the car and we walked toward the main entrance where Pastor Jimmy was chatting with his dad and a couple of church members. Kay's left arm was inside my right arm, and we approached them with welcoming smiles although I was fearful for reasons I wasn't sure of.

I reached out to shake Pastor Jimmy's hand and we bear-hugged. I already knew what I was going to say. "Hey, Jimmy. You got a sec?"

He said, "Sure" and we moved to a quieter place so I could tell him what was on my mind. In a haunting echo of words I had heard before, he said, "So Ken, what can I do for you?"

If you remember, the last time he said that to me I exploded in hate and wanted to punch him in the face, at the very least. This time, I said meekly, "Jimmy, I said some terrible things thirteen years ago including taking God's name in vain regarding our church. Can you please forgive me for that outburst? I have begged God's forgiveness. But for all these years, it has still weighed heavy on my heart."

He said, "Of course." Then led us in a short prayer, bear-hugged again and that was that. Following a cheerful goodbye after services, we never saw him again.

God had given me a UNIQUE opportunity to seek out forgiveness for the terrible and hurtful things I had said thirteen years before. Coincidence? I don't think so. I believe the Holy Spirit works in fabulously intricate ways that can be very surprising and a huge blessing at the same time.

Less than a year later, we learned Pastor Jimmy was admitted to the hospital with a severe case of pancreatitis. After only four days in the hospital, he died at the young age of forty-two. To say that I was stunned is an understatement. And yet, I marveled at God's plan and His compassion for what we had all gone through in 1987. I still marvel to this day that He gave me such an opportunity to renew the spiritual relationship I had damaged so many years earlier. I was sad for Pastor Jimmy's parents and his loved ones and prayed for their emotional recovery. I never told them what their son had almost pulled off, but I think they probably knew anyway.

+++

"Flipping and flopping like a flying fish on the foredeck of Fidelity."

Now, we time trip back to 1988 and San Diego. There was good news and bad news. First the good news:

One very cool thing happened while I was working at KyXy. I was selected to be the first American deejay to broadcast western style music in China. President Ronald Reagan made the introduction to the program. It was a big deal with potentially well over a billion listeners! A brief recording of the introduction to the program (in Chinese and English) is on the www.culturejock.net website.

CULTURE JOCK

KyXy's Kenny Noble Reaches audience of 1.1 Billion.

BEJING – Kenny Noble of KyXy has been selected the first of 52 American disc jockeys to be spotlighted on the "American Music Hour," the first radio program of American pop music to air in the People's Republic of China in history. A copy of Kenny's history-making broadcast was infused into the Smithsonian Institute.

Airing on the Central People's Broadcasting network to an audience of over 1.1 billion listeners, the one-hour, twice-weekly radio program will present a variety of American music and artists, highlighted by a pre-taped introduction from each of the selected U.S. deejays of their city and a specially selected American song to follow.

Kenny Noble is the KyXy morning show host, weekdays 6 to 10 a.m. Originally from Houston, Kenny has worked in radio for 16 years. He's been honored as Billboard magazine's "Air Personality of the Year," entertaining audiences in Chicago, Seattle and Los Angeles. But Kenny's "Dream Job"? To do mornings at KyXy!

Kenny isn't wasting time on the clutter that most radio stations circulate in the morning: no tactical phone calls or meandering studio dialogue... with Kenny, there's "No Bull" in the morning! Instead, there's music... lots of soft favorites to make people feel good. And when the music stops, there's important information: up to date weather, traffic and news.

Kenny joined KyXy in 1987 as afternoon drive personality. He resides in San Clemente with his wife and two teenage daughters.

The "American Music Hour" premiered April 14, 1988 and featured the historical debut of a number of artists and songs including this year's Academy Award-winning best song, "I Had The Time Of My Life," from the motion picture "Dirty Dancing." Other artists featured included Huey Lewis & the News, John Denver, Dionne Warwick, George Benson, Michael Jackson, Dolly Parton and Glenn Miller, among others.

KyXy Morning Host, Kenny Noble

The first show opened with an international greeting and welcome from President Ronald Reagan in which he hailed the landmark program as an "important cultural exchange between two great nations."

The "American Music Hour" was made possible through an exclusive agreement with the official China Broadcasting Service Corporation.

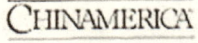
CHINAMERICA

And the bad news? Oh no, not again!! 1991, San Diego. Here's how it went down.

I'm sure getting fired or let go happens differently for people based on their industry. But in the radio industry, the very worst moment in one's career is when the program director pops their head into the studio and says, "Hey, (Kenny) would you mind stepping into my office when you get off the air?" "Uh... sure." As you probably know by now, I had a lot of experience with those type of conversations.

By 1990 I had left KyXy for competitor KJQY and a handsome salary increase! I was one of the first morning hosts in San Diego to use a computer as part of my show and as a source of information for lifestyle topics, interesting news items and funny bits. I had a Radio Shack Tandy computer mounted on a swivel boom for easy access while I was sitting at the studio console. It was connected to a brand-new search engine called Prodigy— an early form of the internet.

I was working about my job, merrily, I might add, for about a year and a half when suddenly they hired a new program director, Jeremy Smith. New management was never a good sign in the radio industry, at least not in my experience, and this guy was extra... what do the young people say today... *'Karen'* about things? ('Karen' is slang for 'obnoxious, angry or, entitled.') He was from New Jersey and had a harsh east coast attitude that just wasn't jiving with our chill west coast vibe. I tried being nice to him, but he wouldn't have it.

For whatever reason, he had it out for me. Along with the overnight deejay, Joe Curtis, whom he never even met! He was always picking apart our shows and telling us all the things we were doing wrong. I suspected the GM wanted us out and now had a new program director to do his dirty work.

Curtis got so tired of Jeremy Smith's intimidating notes that he began to respond with intimidating notes in return. Which I'm pretty sure is why Jeremy decided to show up and surprise Joe one night as he was on the air. Joe worked the late-night shift, so Jeremy really had to go out of his way to be present while Joe was at work.

They began a shouting match which ended when Joe cold-cocked Jeremy right in the face. Joe was of course fired, but that wouldn't be the first 'punchline' involving Jeremy Smith.

The next day, Smith called me into his office. Joe and I were friends, so I had already been tipped off as to what had happened the previous evening. As I walked into his office and took note of Smith's new 'shiner', it took everything inside of me not to acknowledge what was obvious to us both. I already knew what happened and had my suspicions as to what would be happening next, there was no need to add additional fuel to the fire.

Jeremy Smith fired me that day.

There were many times I was let go but I must admit this one stung, and I wasn't even the one who had been punched. He gave me zero opportunities to be nice, just plain cold.

Well, as I said, there was another punchline involving Jeremy Smith which simmered for around eight years. In 1999, I was hosting the morning show with Teri Griffin for Coast 97.3 WFLC in Miami. We worked in a three-story building in Hollywood, Florida. I remember Teri and I had gotten onto the elevator so we could head up to the third floor and talk with the general manager, Bob Greene. I don't recall what we were going to talk to him about but what I do recall is who I saw the moment the elevator doors opened... Jeremy Smith!

After a few minutes of idle chit chat, I asked him what he was doing in the building. He glanced at me and then, with some reluctance I might have been imagining, told me he had applied for a job. In that brief moment, I felt as if I had the upper hand. Nobody at the station would have asked me whether I thought he should be hired but it was a great moment of truth.

If someone had asked me, despite our differences, I would have given him a good word. Life's just too short to hang on to those kinds of differences. He was after all, a single parent and raising his daughter in Miami. In any case, he didn't get the job. And shortly thereafter, I got the sad news he had passed away. I heard he had a heart attack. He was in his early 40s. I am convinced that kind of thing happens more often in broadcasting, for reasons we've already discussed, than it does in most other professions. Sad.

+++

Back to our chronology, you'll recall I was let go by Jeremy Smith in 1991, leaving me unemployed for almost two years! I worked as a freelance videographer most of that time. Very satisfying work, but it didn't pay very well. I needed a real job. And I desperately wanted to get back into radio.

In June of 1993, I was named Program Director at KAFF in Flagstaff, Arizona. I loved Flagstaff, but the job paid so little that we were barely able to stay afloat. There was nothing left over for fun or eating out or anything.

Guy Christian, the owner/general manager, was running things. I can't really blame him because after all, it was HIS small business, but the truth is, owners should hire good people and let THEM do the work while the owner plays golf with the clients or some such recreation.

Mr. Christian turned out to be a micro manager and we didn't really get along that well. Plus, the staff genuinely hated me because I was a major market pro. What they didn't understand is that I was looking to downsize and work in a smaller market so that I could breathe and enjoy life. None of the jocks at KAFF had ever worked in a major market so all they knew was the hustle and bustle of a college town which doesn't compare to working in a major market. They all thought I was there to laud my laurels over them. Good grief, nothing could have been farther from the truth. But the truth was, they made my life miserable. I had to get out of Flagstaff—such a beautiful community. And we loved the church there. I sent out several tapes and resumes to job openings listed in radio trade magazines.

Enter Ross Block, program director at KRWM Seattle. He liked my tape. He liked my resume and he hired me! WOOHOO! "We're going back to Seattle honey!" This time, I wouldn't let a little rain dampen my spirits. Besides, Seattle was now *Latte Central!* YES!! I love espresso and we were moving to the heart of steamed milk and roasted arabica bean country.

I began my second tour of duty in Seattle as morning host at Warm 107. Frank Shiers was my co-host and a guy who was a news pro's pro. Plus, we clicked and got along like guys and TV remotes. It was good times in the Northwest's version of Beantown.

But after about a year, the morning show at KRWM underwent a bit of a shakeup. Co-host Frank Shiers was relegated to movie reviews and such while local newscaster Kathy Golden was given the job of reading the news. Kathy was your classic no-nonsense, no sense of humor news reader. I could tell she was a little uncomfortable with me, but I thought once we got to know each other better, she would loosen up. But no. Kathy was as tight as a rusty nut.

So, there was this full size, cardboard stand-up sign of Spock that was in the lobby of the KRWM studios along the Elliott Bay waterfront in Seattle. It was promoting the latest Star Trek movie, 'Generations.' Set that aside for a moment.

On this socked-in morning, it was foggy all over the Puget Sound area. I had seen a Maidenform bra commercial on TV and decided to have some fun with the forecast. I said, "It looks like we've got 'Maidenform' fog this morning which means that by 10am or so, it should lift and separate." I said that following one of Kathy's newscasts. Her mouth was agape, and she acted offended. I mean good grief; this thing blew way out of proportion because she didn't support my humor. If she felt that way, decent and professional protocol would have been to tell me about it OFF-THE-AIR. But no... Now I was compelled to discuss on the air. Something I really didn't want to do.

So, I gave listeners who called in a chance to sound off and they mostly agreed with me that it was innocent fun, but then a whole cadre of staid listeners thought I was being sexist. That's Seattle for you. Certainly, Kathy was offended that I was being chauvinistic, and she said as much on the air. Well, I *was* being sexist, but I wasn't hateful. To me, it was all in good fun. And I was also poking fun at my own sexism. I never took any of it seriously.

In any case, I was reprimanded. I apologized and the incident was allegedly over.

Except... I had to get even.

Baron, a college-age intern on the morning shift, suggested I might want to place the Spock stand up sign in one of the stalls in the ladies' room and just wait for nature to take its course. This sounded WONDERFUL. So, I quietly slipped the Spock stand up sign in one of the stalls as Baron suggested and waited. It was risky... because there were three stalls. Would Kathy choose door #1, #2 or #3? We were counting on Door #3. It was early, so no one was at the radio station yet. I was stealthy but probably looked somewhat suspicious as I carried Spock like I would a surfboard under my right arm.

Anyway, we waited and waited. Eventually, Kathy said she would 'be right back.' Baron and I looked at each other with hope written all over our innocent-until-proven-guilty faces. Now, it was only a matter of seconds before... "AIE EEEEEEEEEEEEEEEEEEEEEEEEEEE" was heard reverberating from the ladies' restroom. Thanks to Spock, I had my suh-WEEEEEET revenge. Moral of the story? Lighten up. Life is too short.

Disclaimer: *We live in different times. I have since learned to be significantly more sensitive to these kinds of issues. When it comes to any kind of harassment, I have learned my lesson and it's not about getting even. It's about earning respect.*

+++

Christmas 1994 will always be remembered in Seattle as 'The year we almost rid the Earth of fruitcakes once and for all!' And if not, it should be.

Frank Shiers, morning co-host on KRWM Warm 107, had the brilliant idea to buy back fruitcakes. He was inspired by a local law enforcement program to buy back weapons: side arms, pistols, guns, rifles, blow darts, you name it. Frank believed that by doing something as ridiculously ridiculous as buying back fruitcakes that nobody ever eats but instead just regifts to their older family members, we could accomplish two goals: raise awareness of the gun buyback program and more importantly, eliminate all fruitcakes once and for all.

By the way, the reason we have always regifted fruitcakes to our more senior family members is because we assume they are more likely than younger folks to bite into a fruitcake. But that proved to be false as we learned that fruitcake bias was alive and well across all demos.

What did we buy back the fruitcakes with? Well, certainly not cold cash because we didn't have any. But we did have connections with Cinnabon Cinnamon Rolls. Everyone who returned a fruitcake was rewarded with a certificate for a tasty, uber sweet Cinnabon Cinnamon roll. Cinnabon got tons of publicity, fruitcakes were abandoned in droves and Kenny and Frank basked in the afterglow of a sugar high throughout the holidays.

The program was immensely successful with TV news coverage and a blurb in the Seattle Times. Not only that, it was also fun!!

+++

NOT so much fun, however, was the thought of moving... again. Yeppers. I was let go. And good grief this was getting old. I loved that job, but as luck (and prayer) would have it, I was immediately hired by Rob Edwards at KACD Santa Monica. It was May of '95 and following two years at the helm of KRWM, we were headed south (again) on I-5, by this time all too familiar.

We relocated to Irvine, California (south of L.A.), but... wait for it... after only one year and two months, we moved BACK to Seattle... huh??? Yes, the result of another format flip. When I was hired, KACD was playing the 60s, 70s and 80s. The flip was to dance music. Ugh! (And disco STILL sucks!) So, we just wanted to get back to Seattle because we now loved the area. (And we hungered for I-5 one more time LOL) I really wanted to make it in Seattle, but no. I felt like Moses when God showed him the Promised Land. "There it is Bunky! But you'll never live there permanently", or words to that effect.

By now, I'm guessing your impression of my career is something like, "That Kenny. He's always *flipping and flopping like a flying fish on the foredeck of Fidelity*." Well, whoever said that was right. I ended up having to work three part-time jobs just to make ends meet. Seattle had also received upwards of 30 inches of snow over the Christmas weekend and then, during your basic rainy February chill, and out of the blue, Miami called with a great offer to be the new morning host for $80,000 a year!! What would YOU do? ☺

No brainer. "Honey, we're headed to the beaches of South Florida! *"Cuando caliente el sol en la playa!"* (How hot is the sun on the beach!)

+++

CHAPTER 13

MIRACLE OF MIRACLES

---

*I don't claim to know why one person's time
comes early and another is let to live but I thank
God for knowing I would need Sam.*

It's early spring, 1997 – time to hitch 'em up and haul 'em home to new challenges in the Sunshine State! Our caravan consisted of a 26' U-Haul truck packed to the gills with our stuff and Kay's Honda Accord, also packed but with room for the boys riding with her. The girls were now in their early twenties and had moved out of the house. I was driving the truck following Kay's car. As we started our cross-country journey, I flipped the talk switch on my walkie talkie and said, "I've got your back, honey!"

She replied, "That's a big 10-4, big fella. Let's do this."

We set out through the morning overcast that Seattle, as well as many other coastal communities are known for—a thumbs up and we were on our way to South Florida. That's a long way, folks. We were headed for a new experience, a new job as morning host of Coast 97.3 FM Miami and a rendezvous with a near drowning that came very close to bringing disaster upon us all. But here I go jumping a little ahead again.

We worked our way across the country thanks to Cheez-its and trail mix. As we headed east away from Seattle and across Washington State and Idaho, it was late at night before we crossed into Montana along Interstate 90. And there it was! The comet of the century! The Hale-Bopp comet stole the limelight away from the moon—a stunning appearance that lit up Big Sky country heralding the biggest move of our lives. We pulled over for a break and to gaze at this once-in-a-lifetime celestial event. Hale-Bopp last appeared forty-two *hundred* years ago. So, this was a big deal! We followed it all the way to Miami.

Moving from Seattle to Miami not only made good economic sense, it was also a great job opportunity. Program Director Tip Landay made sure I would be paid well. So even though we preferred Seattle, we decided to give *la vida loca* a chance.

We arrived safe, sound, and tired but four days later, very happy to be in Broward County where we had previously put a deposit on an apartment in Coral Springs—a delightful area with a wonderful pool surrounded by royal palms bordering well-maintained and beautifully landscaped common areas. We would be sure to take advantage of the pool, especially in the warmer months… pretty much all year!

We found a community church right away. There were about three hundred and fifty members—a good size to get to know people, make new friends and being a part of

Bible studies, volunteer efforts, and community projects. We ultimately worshiped there for the entire six years of our stay in beautiful 'SoFla' (South Florida) as it was known locally.

For the most part, life was pretty average for us during the first five months. In September, we found a house to buy but weren't scheduled to close for another thirty days. So, we continued to take advantage of the community pool at our Coral Springs apartment.

In South Florida, water is everywhere. There are hundreds of miles of canals, swimming pools in nearly every backyard or neighborhood, lakes scattered all around town, and, of course, the ocean. So, it came as no surprise that the number one cause of death for children five and under was drowning. Kay and I made sure to enroll the boys in swimming lessons. By this time, they had two weeks' worth of lessons under their belt and, as far as I was concerned, they could swim the English Channel.

Sadly, on September 9, 1997, I would learn that accidents can happen no matter how much one thinks they are prepared.

On this day, I took Sam, 4, and Kenny Jr., 7, to the apartment swimming pool. It was a beautiful, warm South Florida day. Kay stayed back at the apartment to take a nap. In typical, father/son fashion, me and the boys splashed each other and ourselves to oblivion. I got absorbed in the fun as we cavorted around the pool like monkeys. Other families were at the pool as well but it's easy to forget their existence when you're having fun with your boys. Sam could barely touch the bottom in the shallow end but he seemed to be managing. I got distracted lifting and tossing Kenny Jr. into the air. When I looked back to check on Sam, he was nowhere to be seen.

As I rushed toward the last place I had seen him, something at the bottom of the pool caught my attention. There was Sam, face down on the bottom and unconscious. I scooped him up and screamed for someone to call 9-1-1. A nurse and Marine happened to be at the pool and immediately started giving him CPR. Unfortunately, their efforts weren't getting anywhere.

The Coral Springs Fire Department showed up quickly and gave him oxygen. Kay was still back at the apartment completely unaware that our baby's life was on the brink of his existence. Kenny Jr. and I stood by helplessly hoping for some sign of life to appear. I sent Kenny to get his mom!!

And then Sam's eyes popped open as he let out this awful blood curdling scream. It was both terrifying and a relief. The lights were on, nobody was home... but he was alive! They took him to the hospital around 5PM. It wasn't until the next day that he started coming around as himself again.

It was a miracle. I thanked God for saving Sam that day, (and I've thanked Him every day since for giving us Sam twice) thinking that was the end of the event, end of the story. Sam was given a new lease on life, our family had dodged a bullet that day, and life goes on. It would be twelve years later before I would truly realize what God had done that day.

So, let's fast forward for a moment to 2009. I was drinking again; The economy was terrible. I had tried and failed a dozen times to get a loan modification, but I did not have a job and was behind on our house payments for almost a year. After five years with smooth jazz, the station I worked for, KJCD Denver, flipped formats to Sports/Talk and had let me and most of the staff go. That's no excuse to drink, but those were *my* reasons.

Kay and I were once again on shaky ground. She was clear to let me know that *she* knew I was drinking. But I thought I was doing well to hide it from the rest of the family. Little did I know, the boys were not as naive as I thought; they knew exactly what was going on with me. By this time, it had been a year and some change since being let go from KJCD and still didn't have a job.

Sam was now sixteen years old. We decided to have lunch together at a local place that served great buffalo wings. I asked Sam if he minded if I had a beer. (Any excuse for me.) To my surprise, he said, "Yeah, dad, I do mind. Don't do it."

That day, Sam shocked me into reality. His boldness was the catalyst that led to my repentance.

In 1997, I was thanking God for saving Samuel. I was so grateful that he had spared my son to live another day. Little did I know God would use my son to rescue *me* twelve years later. It's a reality that left me speechless, and that's not something I can often claim. God, in all his vast knowledge, can see twelve years down the road and say, "Nope, not today."

I don't claim to know why one person's time comes early and another is let to live but I thank God for knowing I would need Sam.

+++

Sam's near drowning shook our family to the core. The only thing he suffered that day was petechiae (blood vessels bursting). He had closed his eyes so tight that he burst a bunch of blood vessels in his eyelids. So, it was there for a few days and then nothing to show for it but a terrifying memory. As a father, this was one of those memories that would never fade. I was grateful that Kay was spared the sheer horror I had experienced. Today it serves as a reminder of God's goodness and the beautiful way his plans for our lives come together over time.

Following his recovery, I made it a point of discussion on the Coast 97.3 morning show. Teri and I would take listeners, put them on the air and discuss the best way to avoid accidents like that since there's so much water in south Florida. Other than small children, drunks were a category who seemed to be targeted by drowning as well. Someone would decide to drink and drive then soon find themselves in a canal surrounded by water. Or, they would party too hard at the beach and get caught in a riptide. These all became discussion points as we talked through the topic on our show. The moral of the story was, water can be deadly. Watch your kids, stay sober near it, and, oh yeah, don't drink and drive!

As all this important discussion was going on, lightning struck again. Only this time it wasn't *our* family. The family across the street were about to experience their worst nightmare.

We had just moved into our new home, and I came home from work one afternoon to find emergency vehicles and flashing lights parked in front of the neighbor's house. As my blood pressure escalated and my pulse quickened, I walked up to one of the EMTs and asked them what had happened. A young mother was entertaining a friend; her three-year-old daughter wandered into the backyard and slipped into the pool. By the time they discovered her, she had been under the water for several minutes and was beyond help. About this time, the other EMTs wheeled this beautiful little girl out on a gurney. She wasn't covered like they usually show in the movies. Seeing that tiny body lying so still and lifeless on that gurney flooded my mind with memories of Sam's near drowning. Emotionally, it was devastating.

This hit close to home. More than a little too close. I'm pretty sure I hugged Sam extra hard that day.

+++

That Christmas, Kay and I decided to give the boys bicycles. Of course, at age 4 and 7, they didn't know how to ride them. That part was left up to me, ha-ha!

I remember taking the boys out every day for about a week and pushing them – then letting them go and watching them fall. Of course, that was the hard part, but nobody was really hurt. They wore knee pads and helmets which might as well have contained springboards with how quickly they jumped back on their bikes and kept at it. By the end of the week, they got it!! So, a new chapter of mobility had arrived in the Noble family.

I ran three miles every day back then and invited the boys to ride their bikes along with me. I had done the same thing with the girls back around 1980. It was truly emotional for me to be running with my sons 'in tow' on their bikes. I'm not sure if it was the difference in girls vs. boys, or that I was now older and had already completed some major life stages with the girls, but I felt it was very important to teach them 'the ways of the road'.

We stopped at all stop signs and red lights. I had the boys dismount their bikes and walk them across all streets. It was interesting to see the habits they were forming as they learned almost daily how to master bike riding.

In the back of my mind, I noted that someday I might be teaching them how to drive (which I did of course) and I had hoped the way in which they were taught to ride their bikes would transcend the years and be in place when one day 'far off in the future' they would sit behind the wheel of a car. To this day both sons are careful drivers and I like to think that old dad was at least partly responsible.

The writer of Proverbs 22:6, made this statement, *"Direct your children onto the right path, and when they are older, they will not leave it."*

So often it is used specifically to encourage parents to raise their children in the ways of the Lord. But it is sound advice for all parents, Christian or not. For me, it's a reminder that habits which are started when we're young can remain throughout one's lifetime. I am living proof of that principle which works both for good and bad as my addictive personality continues to raise its ugly head.

I suppose in my situation, when speaking of my struggle, some might excuse me with the common saying, "You can't teach an old dog a new trick."

The truth, and we all know it, is that us "old dogs" *can* learn new tricks. It's just not as easy because the further our life gets along the more likely we are to adapt and conform to comfort and familiarity. Get 'em while they're young and raise 'em up right!

+++

Before I continue, I want to touch for a minute on the life of the unemployed. I'm sure by now you might be wondering why anyone would consider a career in radio with so many format flips and ownership changes of hands. It certainly wasn't easy but a good majority of the time I was prepared. I had something else already lined up or saw the changes and got prepared.

Honestly, the broadcasting profession is more like that of a contractor moving from job to job. Few are fortunate enough to stay in one place. Some do. Most of us move, either because we want to or because we must, from one opportunity to the next. Broadcasting is ideal for moving up the ladder because it relies so much on experience, more so than actual qualifications. I was being let go from Coast 97.3 because the guy who hired me was let go. It was one of the few times when there was no preparation and I felt it deeply.

Unemployment has a way of beating one's self-esteem to a pulp while also wreaking havoc on their relationships. For me, I believe this was especially true because I easily found my identity and worth in what I did and where I worked. Losing this felt like life as I knew it was over. What was I good for now? This kind of damage to one's self-esteem is not helpful when you're searching for a job. Potential employers don't want to hear how desperately you need their open position. That's a surefire way to kill the interview. And on top of that, nobody wants someone who is negative or full of despair.

The best thing to do is stay in a positive attitude.

I was not always great at maintaining the positive attitude needed. Instead, I seemed to be comforted by worrying and stressing over my lack of employment. If only I took the advice of Jesus. He told us not to worry but instead trust that God is in control.

The worrying is what caused the biggest strain on my relationships. Young children of course pick up quickly that something is wrong even if you don't tell them. Then, they aren't sure if they too should be worrying or what they should feel since they're not being properly guided. Kay and I were already on shaky ground, so this kind of attitude didn't lend any help. See, when adults encounter someone who is worrying, bitter, or angry they tend to avoid that person. I think it is human nature. We think there is nothing we can do or contribute to help the person, so we avoid them all together.

However, there is something we can do. Just be there for them. That's the biggest lesson I learned from my desperate days of unemployment.

+++

When it came to my job at Coast 97.3, it was the 'same old song. I got fired at WFLC in 2000, this time because the program director who hired me got fired. I knew as soon as Tip was let go; I'd be next – and within two days, I was. I was out of work for about three months and thanks to Clear Channel Ops Manager Rob Roberts, I finally ended up working again, but this time it would be WLVE, LOVE 94, Smooth Jazz in Miami.

I began my three-year 'tour of duty' at LOVE 94 with actress/producer Tara McNamara as co-host/news. She was good, very good. But after a few months, Tara moved on and eventually ended up in Southern California with her own TV show. After Tara, I learned that my wonderful 'partner in crime' from Coast 97.3, Teri Griffin was looking for a job. A call here, an interview there and voila! Teri and I were reunited! I think she was the best co-host of my career.

We got along famously—Teri, the closest thing to the Shell Answer Man on the planet AND a lover of gladiator movies. Me? Well, I was the Roger Murdock of radio, "Huh?"

We were blessed with so many good interviews from Gloria Estefan to Robert Duvall. One of the funniest interviews we ever did was with Leslie Nielsen, who entered our studio laughing. And in true Garrison Keillor form, we also ended up 'laughing so hard' our 'noses whistled'.

> *"Roger, roger. What's our vector, Victor?"*
> *"Surely, you can't be serious?"*
> *"I am serious and don't call me Shirley!"*
> (From the movie, Airplane)

(Links to all three of these interviews at the back of the book)

Those six years divided between Coast 97.3 and Love 94 were some of the best years in my radio career. But nothing lasts forever. We were working for Clear Channel Communications. Their mantra: *Fewer people, more work, less money.* Seriously, I made that up, but it honestly describes the careers of so many pros who by all rights should have been able to retire from that company but were let go instead so that CC could hire employees who would work for less money and far fewer benefits. It was pretty clear to everyone that CC was in competition with itself over the bottom line.

CHAPTER 14

MILE HIGH DREAMS

---

*"For a relationship to work,
we need to work the relationship.*

September 11, 2001, arrived in Miami as shockingly as it did everywhere else in America. I was in the Love 94 control room with about ten minutes left on my morning show. One of the news people at our seven-station Clear Channel cluster came running down the hall shouting, "A plane just crashed into the World Trade Center!!"

I had to get a song started before I could run down to the news center to see what this was all about, but I figured that since an airplane once crashed into the Empire State Building, why would this be any different? I assumed it was probably a similar instance of a plane inadvertently crashing into a building in the fog. Only thing is...

I was wrong. The weather in NYC on September 11 was vibrantly blue and clear.

Little known fact fourteen people died in 1945, when a B-25 Mitchell bomber of the United States Army Air Forces, flying in thick fog, crashed into the Empire State Building in New York City.

And the newsroom TV monitors concurred—it was a crystal-clear morning in New York on 9/11. Everyone was glued to the screens when suddenly a second airplane crashed into the South Tower of the World Trade Center. Everything got surreal after that. It was like a nightmare in real time.

There were two more crashes – the Pentagon taking a direct hit, and the brave passengers aboard a hijacked United flight who stormed the cockpit and caused the terrorists to crash their plane into the ground near Somerset, Pennsylvania. All forty-four people on board including the hijackers were killed. Nobody knew what to think other than...

America was under attack.

I don't know anyone who wasn't glued to their TV sets for weeks after that. Americans were briefly united, and President Bush vowed to hit the terrorists where they lived or where they were hiding. Plans were begun for a memorial for the almost three thousand people who lost their lives on what would now forever be known as 9/11.

It was one of those moments in life where you never forget, even to this day so many years later, where you were when it happened.

+++

On a more pleasant note, one moment I will also NEVER forget goes back to 2002 and my interview with Gloria Estefan! She was just awesome!

While you're on the radio, especially the morning show, there are many opportunities for interviews and no place was better than in South Florida's clear channel cluster. There were seven radio stations all within the same building which made us everyone's top one-stop shop. Teri Griffin and I were exposed to a wide spectrum of guests – everyone from Gloria Estefan to Jeb Bush, the governor of Florida at that time.

Gloria Estefan was one guest I might have been a bit over the top excited to meet. I was interested to see if the personality I had formed in my mind aligned with the real person. She did not disappoint. She was just as kind, warm and bubbly in person as she seemed to be everywhere else. I would have to say she had the best personality of anybody I had ever met. She was especially great at interviews because there was never a moment of dead air. She was talking, I was talking, Teri was talking, she was talking again, and it all flowed seamlessly.

One reason she was so great during the interview? She was an excellent listener. She even had the decency of remembering our names and using them during the conversation. Man, how those simple things can have such a powerful effect.

When Jeb Bush walked into the studio for his interview, I tipped my head back as I thought, *Whoa, he's gigantic!* He had to be at least 6'5" in my opinion. When we asked if he had any presidential aspirations he replied, "Well, I... ah... nope I don't."

I suppose I can relate to having those difficult moments when you're put on the spot while live on air.

After the interview, I asked if I could get a picture with him. When I looked at that picture, I was aghast at the difference in height between us. Good grief, it looked like Frodo standing next to Gandalf! That photo will never see the light of day. My ego just won't allow it, ha-ha! BTW, links to Gloria Estefan's interview and others including Leslie Nielsen and Robert Duvall are at the end of the book.

+++

About a year after this interview, Florida was experiencing a citrus crisis. It was all because of the dreaded citrus canker disease which left affected citrus with some minor discoloration but nothing more. The fruit was fine.

When the fruit pandemic was at its peak Governor Jeb Bush took to the podium and branded individuals with citrus trees on private property to be the bad guys. It was obvious the 'innocent' and uber rich citrus grove owners had far-reaching political gravitas in Florida politics and would be given preference. Meanwhile, the state said they would be sending tree cutters to cut down any citrus trees on personal property that were within a thousand yards of an infected tree. That pretty much wiped out the citrus trees of private owners all over the state. I suppose it was to reduce the spread of citrus canker, but I was not a happy man.

I had always enjoyed planting trees everywhere we moved. And, since I had a soapbox, I openly talked on the morning show about my distaste for this decision. Even going so far as to say, "If they want to cut down my trees, they'll have to arrest me." Since I made such a big fuss, I suppose they thought I would be the best candidate to use as an example for others: "This will be happening regardless of your opinion."

Following a curt phone call from the tree cutters, they showed up at my house within about a half hour. They were accompanied by the sheriff. But what they weren't prepared for was the TV crew I had tipped off that arrived seconds before them. I was bound and determined they were going to have to haul me off to jail or cut the tree down with me up in it. It was a violation of my rights, and I wasn't going to be pushed around by the State.

The sheriff took a deep breath reminiscent of Sheriff Buford T. Justice that puffed out his chest before he walked over to me and calmly stated, "You need to let me inside your property." Now that I think about it, he probably had much better things to do with his day but kudos to him for remaining calm with my tree hugging self.

"I can't do that." I replied. And as anger began welling up within me, I turned, looked straight into the camera, then passionately and patriotically affirmed, "Jeb Bush, you can't do this. This isn't Cuba, it's the United States of America!"

I'm not sure what had come over me in that moment, but it has given my friends and family ammunition to mock me at every opportunity as they often quote, "This isn't Cuba!"

The sheriff calmly leaned towards me and quietly said, "You made your point. You're on TV. Do you really want me to arrest you over a tree?" Kay was standing off to the side shaking her head, an excellent prompt that it just wasn't worth it.

They cut down five of my trees that day which was a sad moment. However, there was a class action lawsuit brought against the state by the united homeowners of Florida. The court ruled in our favor and the state was required to pay $90 for every tree they cut down on private property. I still would have rather had my trees instead but at least the justice system gave us a victory of sorts. I wondered if they had caught my Cuba comment on the news?

+++

Once again, all good things had come to an end. Teri eventually moved on and now can frequently be found on Friday nights face down in a platter of oysters Rockefeller at one of the many seafood restaurants and oyster bars in Ft. Myers, Florida where she has retired to live in chicken fried splendor.

In the summer of 2003, I sent a tape and resume to Denver for a smooth jazz opening in the Mile High City. Because I had three solid years of smooth jazz experience, I had an edge over most other applicants and was hired.

While at Clear Channel in Miami, I had been working with our news person, Simone Seikaly for a couple of years and we had become good friends. When we moved to Denver in 2003 to work for KJCD 104.3, I learned that Simone had ALSO applied for a news position at KJCD, and she was hired too! Simone moved a week or two before we did and because she didn't have room to bring some furniture items with her, we were able to bring some of her stuff with us when we moved a few days later.

Both Simone and I would be working with Smooth Jazz 104.3 Program Director Michael Fischer. He expected, demanded, and got positive results. I appreciated the work environment he created at Jefferson-Pilot. He was a pro to the max and a lot of fun on remote broadcasts, especially the ones in Mexico!

But... during the very first week of my job, I put a listener on the air who badmouthed our competition—KOSI 101 FM. I had done this kind of bit pretty much everywhere I had worked. The listener, who was not prompted, not only said she couldn't stand KOSI ('Cozy') but LOVED Smooth Jazz 104.3. To me it was a no-brainer. To Michael, I was a no-jobber. He was furious and said he was going to let me go but had to think about it first. During his 'thinking' time I raced to the local liquor store and purchased a fine bottle of wine with a larger-than-life card that said how S-O-R-R-Y yes, V-E-R-Y sorry I was. Fortunately, that soothed his savage beast and we 'were good' again. Whew! I mean we had just hung our pictures up at the apartment! Desperate times call for desperate measures, but it was worth it. Close call.

Our family found a great church in Lakewood about the same size as our church in South Florida. The people were friendly, caring, and compassionate. The singing and the music were heavenly. We had found a church home that would serve us well for the next fifteen years!

The five years I worked for Smooth Jazz 104.3 were fulfilling years topped off with remote Mexico broadcasts from Ixtapa/Zihuatanejo, Baja California and many cool locations around Denver including Fiddler's Green Amphitheater in Greenwood Village and Red Rocks Amphitheater near Morrison where we hosted several big-name smooth jazz artists for awesome concerts. There were after work listener parties, summer and winter jazz festivals, and wine tastings.

Oh yeah, did I mention wine tastings? By now you know, I didn't miss any of those. My old addictive nemesis had returned to haunt me again. The wine flowed freely and abundantly. I was headed for another disaster that would take about five years to incubate. (Keep in mind, it was still a few more years before Sam would hit me with bold comments.)

I ended up working for KJCD until 2008. I was very excited to be working for them and then it happened again—format flip to sports/talk. A year before they flipped, they gave me an intern to work with me. Most of the time, people think of interns as young, fresh out of college kids who either lack confidence or have enough confidence to fill a stadium. Jamie was neither of those stereotypes. She was a very capable, attractive, and talented young single woman in her 40s. She had gone to broadcast school and was ready to work in the field. We worked very closely with one another in the cramped KJCD studio. She was a hard worker. I relied on her for so much and found myself frequently thinking about her.

My feelings for her led to an emotional affair.

She, of course, didn't have a clue until I started calling her after drinking a beer or two and I picked up what seemed like the Enemy's favorite pastime—that is, ME doing lots of stupid things. It never ceases to amaze me how evil changes its appearance and its M-O to deceive in new and creative ways, for example, "Yeah, it's okay to drink because I've had a bad day and I need a pick-me-up." Or some other such rubbish.

One of the stupid things I would do would be to call Jamie while Kay was at work. Instead of finding stuff around the house to do or picking up a hobby, here I was losing my focus on her and returning to old and dangerous habits. I knew these feelings were inappropriate. It's just that Jamie really enjoyed my company, she showed me a lot of respect and that's important to a man. We enjoyed talking with each other. (So that made it alright, buddy?) I had these inappropriate feelings towards her, and I finally let her know. I didn't say anything that was overt, but I was a little too cozy with our emails and what we would say back and forth.

I was reluctant to take it further, but I was getting respect and admiration which I was not receiving from Kay. We had slowly drifted apart... again. Any sane person would say this has no good ending to it. But the alcohol was convincing me otherwise.

In June of 2008, I lost my job as a result of the format switch to sports/talk. I had more free time and started drinking more and calling Jamie more frequently. Life took a turn for the worse when Kay discovered my emails with Jamie. She threw stuff at me. I had it coming for sure. She was livid and her anger really WAS fire and brimstone. It was all I could do to duck.

The only thing I did say was, "I never once touched this woman. I didn't kiss her or hold hands or anything like that."

I just had an emotional attachment with her. I knew it was wrong and I was at fault. I told Kay I would break it off. I felt badly about it because I knew Jamie didn't completely understand. I mean, it was MY emotional affair, not hers. She said, "Why can't we be friends?"

Not possible. Kay demanded total compliance which meant cutting off all communications with her, cold turkey, getting rid of all files, emails, photos, and everything associated with her. There was NO chance we could be friends... AT ALL! I was embarrassed to admit all this to Jamie, but I did what I had to do.

Kay calmed down, but the damage had been done and she began to fantasize about leaving me. I know that because several years later, I found a counseling questionnaire folded up in a shoebox of old photos. It was hard to read. I didn't know she felt that way at the time, and it hurt, but I was hardly surprised. Relationships are tenuous when they are not 'watered' and 'groomed.'

For a relationship to work, both parties need to work the relationship. The traditional marriage vows set the tone for it all "...to have and to hold from this day forward, for better, for worse, for richer, for poorer, in sickness and in health, to love and to cherish, till death do us part..." Whoever first came up with those words understood the commitment of marriage would take a lot of... well commitment.

Sadly, after finding that questionnaire, I felt some familiar feelings trying to undermine our marriage. The Enemy was on the prowl... again!

+++

CHAPTER 15

RECKONING AND REDEMPTION

"We lost our deposit but found our lives."

My drinking continued and because I was out of work, it became worse. My life was unraveling. We couldn't make our house payments; unemployment just wasn't enough to pay all the bills and any attempt at getting a loan modification was met with indifference and downright apathy. The next two years were indeed rugged, but a couple of things happened to reverse our direction. One, more than any other!

As mentioned earlier, our son Sam confronted me about my alcoholism around this time. It was 2009 and I needed to do something about almost everything. That's how bad it was. Or as comedy writer *Don Adams* once said, "I was so far behind I thought I was in first!" So, I did the only thing left to do that made any sense at all—*I repented of my addiction and threw away the 'bottle.'* I rid our home of all alcohol and began a 'new' way of life. I felt like Moses after he came down from the mountain and found his people worshipping a gold calf. God was back in the building! And me?

I was sober.

Out of the blue, I got a job!!!

Not just any job, but as a news reporter/producer/anchor with the K-LOVE and Air1 Radio Networks! I had applied a year earlier but had not heard anything. So, I was shocked when their HR department manager called and said, "Kenny, we have two openings at K-LOVE that we believe you are qualified for. One is an air talent position here in Rocklin, California and the other is a local news position in Denver."

Seemed like a no-brainer, I didn't have money to move and was already in Denver. So, you guessed it, I chose Denver.

All I had ever done in radio was deejay work. There was a place on the clock I needed to be every minute for four hours Monday through Friday. But now, I would be doing assignment work. Bring it on! I would be using the same technical toolbox but in an entirely different way. I was ready for the change and certainly ready to go to work for a Christian organization. Amen!!

My expectations were pretty high, and K-LOVE did not fail to meet those standards. I had hoped that being around a similar environment at church, work, and home would starve out my thirst for the world. It did not, but thankfully was held more in check. And for that, I am grateful. When I interviewed for the position at their corporate headquarters, I could instantly sense this would be different from any radio station I had worked for in the past. It was a 'kinder, gentler' atmosphere.

I excelled at it and really liked it. Ed Lenane, a consummate pro with an awesome voice, was my hiring manager. When Ed transferred to K-LOVE and Air1's Indianapolis operations, Richard Hunt took over the news supervisor reins. He turned out to be the best program director I ever worked for. He was and still is an absolute jewel of a people person and when it comes to the nuts and bolts, Richard Hunt is a newsman's newsman.

Meanwhile I hadn't been making house payments.

I had tried numerous times to get a loan modification, but the value of our home had gone down significantly in 2008 when the market crashed so nobody wanted to work with me. We made a deposit on an apartment and put our house up for short sale. It was officially on the market for only four days when I received a call from CitiMortgage. Our new loan payment was only going to be $40 more than what we were about to pay for the apartment we had put the deposit on! We lost our deposit but found our lives.

Wow! When God answers prayer, he puts on a show!

What a blessing my repentance was in every area of my life and by extension, my family's lives. When I finally retired from radio in late 2016, we were able to do so from the money we made off selling our house. Between 2014 and 2018, Denver real estate took off like an Elon Musk rocket. Thank you, God! And thank you Dave Ramsey for putting us on a cash-only course two years earlier.

+++

Sometimes, it is hard to recognize and appreciate the blessings we are given because they're blended in among lows and hardships.

+++

In 2013, our youngest son Samuel invited me to climb one of Colorado's 58 14ers. For those of you who don't know, 14ers are mountains that reach 14,000 plus feet above sea level. For this father-son adventure, he had chosen La Plata which towers to 14,367 feet above sea level—third highest peak in Colorado.

You'll recall, it had only been a little more than three years since Sam had rescued me from myself by confronting me about my alcoholic addiction. That had truly been a valley moment in our relationship, so I jumped at the opportunity to experience this, literal, mountaintop moment with him.

Sam took charge of the trip and laid out our itinerary.

La Plata was about two hours away from our home in Lakewood. We would leave around 8pm and drive to the trailhead which was about 10,000 feet above sea level. The plan called for us to camp out overnight and then head out to the summit via the trailhead around 4am. It was important to get to the top and back down again before early afternoon when thunderstorms are at their greatest danger to climbers. Nobody wants to be caught out in the open while numerous lightning strikes are occurring on an exposed mountain.

Before the camp was set up, I looked up at the amazing crystal-clear sky and for the first time in my life witnessed the awesome Milky Way! OMG, it was truly one of God's greatest creations. Such beauty in the sky kept my eyes staring not only at the countless stars but Sam had timed our visit to coincide with the annual Perseid meteor shower! The 'Big Show' just got bigger with multiple meteors per minute streaking across a stunning vista. It was mind-blowing.

Neither of us got more than a few hours of sleep that night. For one thing, the air at 10,000 feet is thin which creates the tendency to wake up frequently just to take a deep breath. After some quick camp coffee (so acidic it could melt the chrome right off a 57 Chevy bumper) we headed out as planned at 4am with flashlights and backpacks containing water and snacks. It takes a person in excellent health about three hours to climb the final four thousand feet of mountain before reaching the top. Sam could have easily done it. As I'm writing this, he has summited thirty-five of Colorado's beautiful 14ers. But instead, he hung back with his old dad, and we made it to the top in five hours of heavy breathing and awe-inspiring views.

That mountaintop experience was certainly a humbling one for me. Taking in God's amazing creation at such heights was breathtaking. But what amazed me even more, was glancing at my son while we were on the summit, and in that moment realizing all that God had done just to make this one special moment possible. It is that which left me speechless.

+++

CHAPTER 16

SAVING THE BEST FOR LAST

"Everyone doesn't always get along, but there's an unstated principle in effect that says, "Hey, we're all Christian brothers and sisters here and let's not forget our mission… to save souls."

How could I possibly have known that a career with more twists and turns than an Olympic gymnast, would end with the *best* job out of my forty-three years of radio broadcasting?

Well, for one thing, I had less than a three-mile commute to the K-LOVE Denver offices and studio. Back in SoCal, I commuted to Los Angeles for five years – sixty-six miles each way from San Clemente. The following four years I worked in San Diego. That drive was *only* fifty-five miles each way. I went through cars like cops go through donuts averaging almost fifty thousand miles per year!

My daily prayer was, "Dear God, please bless me with a job, home and church in the same community." And he did just that! We lived, worked, and worshiped in Lakewood. God is awesome!

Secondly, I made the 'time' leap to assignment work. I noted earlier that as a deejay, I had an inflexible, unforgiving clock that pinned me to it every minute of every hour for four hours, Monday through Friday. There was ALWAYS something requiring my attention. That kind of focus is stressful, and, by the way, that's why on-air shifts are, generally speaking, only four hours. Hard to keep up that kind of mental energy for longer periods. Especially during the busy morning and afternoon drive shifts— your basic juggling acts of radio. Successful AM and PM drive jocks typically shuffle weather, traffic, news, lifestyle reports, bits, and special guests with a dazzling display of alacrity. The rest of the workday is usually spent off the air either preparing for the next day, producing commercials, recording, and/or mixing down various audio assignments including interviews, promos, or special station events.

The difference between deejay air shifts and news assignments is night and day. As a newsperson, I would receive an assignment like the Japan earthquake and tsunami in 2011 for example. That story needed first to be sketched out. There might be audio to record from a spokesperson which would require a recorded phone call or Skype session. Then, the audio and/or the video from those recordings would need to be edited down to salient points, but not so much that the story is incomplete or leaves unanswered questions.

Each piece of audio or video would need to be set up in the overall writing of the story and that takes time. Which is why stories are assigned in advance where practicable. Obviously, *breaking news* requires writing at breakneck speed to get the story on the air ASAP. Network cut-ins were frequently required where local stories might have national import or interest—severe storms, tornados, earthquakes, floods, and so on.

For me, sitting at my desk first thing in the morning with a fresh cup of French roast coffee, hands, and fingers at the ready to write my story was well, just the best. AND I didn't have to get up a couple of cracks before dawn, either. That was the VERY best part.

The years between 2010 and 2016 were mostly good years for Kay and me. We had a little extra income, and we ate out more frequently and generally saw each other more often. I could drive the six miles to the Lakewood church where Kay was the office manager in ten to fifteen minutes. We could go to lunch together, chat and get caught up on not only church happenings but also the things we needed to do around the house. We talked a lot. They were rewarding days. Our relationship began to blossom again.

I would fly out to K-LOVE headquarters in Rocklin, California (near Sacramento) a couple of times a year. I was always treated like a team member, which I was of course, but I was working remotely in Denver – one of three such local news positions within the network including Kansas City and Indianapolis.

The encouragement we all received from one another was off the charts. And there was corporate prayer every morning streamed live from Rocklin. It was a much-needed break from the usual stresses that arise from jobs that have people issues. Everyone doesn't always get along, but there's an unstated principle in effect that says, "Hey, we're all Christian brothers and sisters here and let's not forget our mission… to save souls."

The K-LOVE years were the absolute best of my career. There was respect and genuine concern for all our souls, especially those of our millions of listeners. With radio stations in every major market, and most medium markets, EMF (Educational Media Foundation's K-LOVE and Air1) was the team to beat for competing contemporary Christian radio networks.

+++

I retired in 2016. Kay retired in 2018, the year we moved to Georgia. After completing forty-three years of radio broadcasting, I'm sure you might be wondering where I landed with my two-step dance; one step in, one step out. Well, I will say that working for K-LOVE/Air1 and retiring there was a Godsend. Yes, I recognized that he opened the door for this opportunity when I was in desperate need for a job but once again, I was only taking into consideration what was happening in the present, not realizing he could see much, MUCH further down the road.

As I briefly mentioned in the last chapter, this radio station was very different from the other stations I had worked for. Rock stations can get quite vulgar at times but anytime I'd visit the corporate office for K-LOVE I'd never be subjected to dirty jokes or foul language. That's not to say all of us were saints and super holy. It was simply an unspoken expectation. We were a Christian radio station, as such, we should walk the walk. And we did.

The green room at K-LOVE was visited regularly by Christian artists who had stopped by for on-air interviews, but instead of having fridges filled with booze to schmooze there were inspirational scriptures written all over the walls. The atmosphere really sets the tone and, like I said, for me this was a Godsend. And besides, frequently there were brownies, coffee cake and always, always fresh coffee. Yum!

Life had already thrown us many twists and turns but one of the biggest seemed to come May 3, 2020. Kay was diagnosed with glioblastoma brain tumors, an abnormally aggressive form of brain cancer. We had just moved to the North Georgia Mountains in Blue Ridge and Kay was keeping her promise to see a doctor about numbness in her left forearm, hand, and foot. Unbelievably, she had a seizure in the medical building parking lot where her appointment was scheduled. A CT scan revealed two tumors about the size of golf balls in the right parietal and temporal lobes of her brain.

The tumors were resected over two craniotomies four weeks apart. She was given 27 of 30 radiation and chemo treatments. The chemo did a number on Kay's white blood cell count. That led to an ER visit the night of August 3 for a platelet transfusion. While at the ER, and possibly caused by her chemo, Kay suffered cardiac arrest.

It took at least ten minutes to get her heart beating again. During this time, she was given oxygen through a manual resuscitator. Her brain did not receive any oxygen for several minutes. The damage was done. She suffered severe anoxia and today languishes in her bed as a quadriplegic. I am her caregiver and it's the hardest job I've ever had, but I am filled with love for my awesome wife. This is a life I never would have chosen, but it's rewarding on so many levels. God chose it for me and because he has, there are seen and unseen blessings now and to come.

There are stories throughout the Bible which speak to God preparing people for the future, typically without their knowledge. David protected his father's sheep from lions and bears but I'm sure he never once considered he'd one day protect his whole nation from a giant. Whether I realized it at the time or not, there have been moments like this in my own life which have prepared me for my current season of life.

For instance, back in the early 80s, I remember watching this show produced by the Churches of Christ called, *Herald of Truth*. It featured Harold Hazelip and Batsell Barrett Baxter (what a cool name, huh?). These two men would discuss various topics with a lot of intellectual insight. A habit that Hazelip had formed and mentioned on the show immediately jumped out of the screen and latched onto me— Genesis through Revelation— he'd read through the entire Bible in a year, then he'd pick up a different version of the Bible and do the same thing the next year. That was such a cool concept to me.

So, for the next twelve years, I read through the Bible from beginning to end and each new year I would start over at the beginning with a new version. It required me to wake up earlier than usual to make time for it as I knew with hosting the morning show I'd be way too distracted in the afternoons to focus on this.

An interesting fact that stood out to me in *Book of Eli*, a movie starring Denzel Washington, was his character's mention of the Bible. He had read through the Bible *thirty times* and completely memorized it. I have read through it twenty times and I'm nowhere close to memorizing it. Although a very violent movie, *Book of Eli* portrayed the Bible as the most important book in the world. That was certainly something it got 100% correct with no fictitious fluff!

> *"In all these years I've been carrying it and reading it every day, I got so caught up in keeping it safe that I forgot to live by what I learned from it."* Denzel Washington, *Book of Eli*, 2010

Making a point to read the Word every morning certainly began to reshape my life. Remember when I mentioned guilt being a large part of my religion then how things changed when I met Kay and found myself in need of a Savior? Well, things changed even more when we moved to Denver and started worshipping at the Lakewood church. This church didn't seem to be focused on the legalistic side of Christianity as some churches in the past had been. At the

Lakewood church, they were more focused on Jesus himself. Which makes total sense. Just like in driving, whatever you focus on is where you'll eventually go.

When you're focused on sin, it should be no surprise when you sin. But when you're focused on God, although sin might present itself, you'll be more likely to repent quickly than to try to cover it up and continue in it. Or worse, hold on to it because of guilt. The kind of forgiveness where you forgive and let go was a bit of a game changer for me. Because I am prone to 'beating myself up', it's something I still must remind myself of. And when I do I like to use a colorful analogy that paints a vivid picture! A wise man once said, asking God to forgive our sins— letting go and letting God, is like dropping your keys into a river of molten lava—

"Let 'em go, 'cause man, they're gone!"

Reading the Bible certainly made me think more about the choices I was making. It probably prepared me for that second encounter with Pastor Jimmy. My heart was in a much different place than it had been before. But more than anything it prepared me for the current storm I'm facing.

I wish I could say, "All this Bible reading has done me so much good that I never sin anymore in any way." But I can't. Eventually, I decided to slow down on my Bible reading. While it was great to accomplish reading through the Bible, I realized it was more important to read it, think about it, and let it sink down into me a little deeper. It's all well and good to know things and remember things but it's the things that penetrate and soften our hearts that really shape who we are.

More than anything, I wish I could say, "I'm 100% sober and haven't had a drink in decades…" or words to that effect. But the truth is that I still struggle. Even more than that, I struggle with the fact that this is even a struggle. Come on, man, after going to church most of my life and reading the Bible cover to cover twenty times shouldn't I have reached sainthood by now or something? Why do I have this thorn in my side, the crutch that I lean on when the world is just a little much to bear? Obviously, if I knew the answer, I wouldn't still be struggling.

There have been long periods of alcoholic drought—a good thing for sure! Twice I have gone four to six years without a drop and even made it to seven years in the 80s. With God's help, I believe it can happen again. But sadly, upon becoming Kay's caregiver on August 20, 2020, I also returned to my addiction.

I'm not proud nor happy about it. There could possibly be serious damage to my liver or pancreas if I keep this up. My doctor has been quite vocal about me quitting. That's the goal. And I am making progress!!

As I reflect on my non-alcoholic years, Kay and I were happiest then. We became even better friends and much closer together during our many trips to Canton for radiation treatments—an hour and fifteen minutes away.

We talked.

We laughed.

We cried.

We prayed.

We listened to and sang along with classic rock and oldies music. And Kay loved to show off her passenger seat dancing. Oh yeah. From the hips up and while buckled in, she would twist and shake, flailing her arms in tune to whatever song with a beat was inspiring her and then she would look flirtingly at the people we drove past on the highway. We just smiled at each other. It was great fun and revealed so much about her sparkling personality.

On the surface, it's hard not to characterize Kay's current situation and by extension, mine, as physically dire, but I am hopeful. I trust in Jesus because I know he knows we need a miracle. And baby step by baby step, we could be on our way as the brain slowly restores and reroutes neural pathways to perform simple tasks. Kay is now able to communicate in limited ways via her eyelids and that is a significant development. God is good and I am confident we'll get through this.

We managed to get through our 50th wedding anniversary on June 4. It was anything but traditional. Since Kay was mostly catatonic, unresponsive, and quadriplegic, she really wasn't a part of the celebration. But we tried. I got her roses and decorated her room with balloons. The nurses and CNAs from hospice were invited and they all came, and they brought more flowers. We had champagne, music from the 70s and a couple of video tributes that I put together and played on the big screen. We had a large, beautiful white wedding cake. It was decorated with "Happy 50th Anniversary to Ken and Kay." We sang the 'Happy Anniversary' song in Kay's makeshift hospital room, and we had fun. Then everybody left and I cried.

+++

The elephant in the room is her glioblastoma. Good news, her cancer is in remission. The bad news? It is still there and could return at any time. None of our doctors has seen anyone with this type of cancer survive more than five years. Not one.

We hope Kay will be the first.

+++

Forty-three years came and went SO fast. When I first started in this industry, I had no idea all the many paths it would take me or where I would end up when I retired in 2016. As legendary play-by-play announcer for the Dodgers, the late Vin Scully, once put it, "It's a mere moment in a man's life between an All-Star game and an old-timer's game."

Sharing these memories with you has been such a great privilege and pleasure. I appreciate your support of *Culture Jock: One Foot in The World, One Foot in The Church*. When I first started writing I wasn't sure how all this would turn out. When you've lived as long as I have there's a lot of stories to sort through. Which ones will make the cut and which ones will end up on the editing floor? Which ones do I want to share, and which ones should never see the light of day? All of the events in this book are true; some names have been changed to protect individuals' identities. After all, as someone who has had their own share of shortcomings, I didn't want to spotlight anyone else's.

This might be the end of the book but like they say on the radio, "There's never time for dead air. When someone takes a breath it's time to jump in and keep the conversation going."

I've still got quite a few stories left in me, but unfortunately, it's time for a commercial break...stay tuned for the next segment to come... *Culture Jock II: (One foot on Earth, the other in Heaven!)*

+++

ACKNOWLEDGEMENTS

My Jesus is at the top of the list of acknowledgments. Without Him, there would be no war within me fighting for my very soul because I would have been lost so long ago. I thank Kay's family—Mitch and Sharon, Rick and Sheila, Pam and Bill, and Damon and Sheley, as well as Amber, Reesa and Moriah for keeping in touch during the most challenging time of our lives.

I also wish to thank my immediate family for all their support and love: Shari and Byron, Mandi and Todd, Emmaline, Cameron, Brody and Hannah, Kenny, Jr., Samuel and Irish. They have all made it their mission to visit me and their severely anoxic mom more times than I can count from their homes in Atlanta, Denver, Seattle and Flagstaff.

James 'Jim' Crews seriously encouraged me to write a book to leave as a legacy for my family. Thanks Jim! You da man!

My sister Sandra and her husband Jim Hammitt have been an enormous source of encouragement praying continually for Kay and me. Thanks to Lawrence and Libby, and Rick and Mary for making me laugh during a particularly difficult time.

Pruitt Hospice CNAs Michelle, Louise, Nancy, Savannah, Becky, Makenzie, Jamisa, Rachel, Allison and Adrianna, served and are serving Kay in ways that make it possible for me to take breaks to write a book! Pruitt nurses Christy, Mariah, Anna, Deborah, Morgan, Theresa, Gina, Lindsy and Jerrod gave me peace of mind that Kay was in good hands. Upper respiratory specialist Alan Chandler, Kelly, and Mike have always been there for me. By sitting with Kay, Bridget made it possible for me to make weekly trips to Walmart. and Annie made it possible to make weekly trips to Tooneys' Open Mic and my Journey Group. Bridget and Annie rock!

Thanks to the hundreds of my colleagues who have assisted me, mentored me and given me strength along the way. Some but not all including Mel Levine, who showed me the 'ropes' of being a deejay in my first job. Tip Landay, who was the epitome of what a program director should be at WFLC Coast 97.3 Miami. Richard Hunt, Senior News Supervisor at the time I was at K-LOVE and Air1 has been one of my biggest cheerleaders. Dave Logan has been such an inspiration to me not only through his own amazing broadcast legacy but his continued support and prayers for Kay.

LaGard Smith inspired me from the beginning with The Narrated Bible many years ago in Santa Monica. Marty and Laurie Crowe, also from SoCal but now back in their first home, Grand Junction, Colorado, have given love and more love.

Thanks to one of my great music heroes, Richie Furay, co-founder of the Buffalo Springfield, pastor and recording artist extraordinaire! Richie has been there with prayers and encouragement all along this difficult path. Producer Darren Rahn has been there with sweet music and sweeter prayers. Saxman Steve Watts is a super prayer warrior! Thanks to comedy writer Don Adams for contributing endless one-liners to my shows over the years (a few even appear in this book!)

KLOVE's Monica, Billie, Kimberley and Marya got it goin' on! Thanks to Laura 'LD' Daniels for her obsession with using correct grammar, her undying support and love. And thanks to Anna Smith for her prayers, visits and especially her faith.

Thanks to Bill Ham and ZZ Top for their early support when I was at KLOL in Houston. Gratitude plus to Rs and Chris, Mike and Kim, Nate "Black Feather" and Michelle, Sam Scales, Tony Chung, and Evan Chavez for all the prayers and support. (You guys may be called on in 'Culture Jock II.' :)

Mil gracias to Program Director Trigger Black at KTFM San Antonio, Tony Raven, Lee Randall and Ken Dowe at KTFM San Antonio and Carolyn Vance, Roy Garcia and Bob Bell who gave me my first job in radio at KORA AM (Now KTAM) Bryan-College Station, Texas.

Bob and Peggy Stevens got me started at Columbia School of Broadcasting. Jackie McCauley at KLOL believed in me as did GM Jerry Lee. Jackie, the first black woman at Rice University, even played 'Sparrow' for Houston listeners on KLOL.

Michael Fischer, PD at KJCD Denver taught me what it was like to not only respect a supervisor but to genuinely like him. Rob Roberts gave me a job when I needed one most. Jay Blackburn hired me as morning host of legendary rock station WLUP Chicago. Sidekick/newsie CARLA LEONARDO provided an edge to the Morning Loop, and she was a good friend.

Jack Popejoy believed in me at KZLA Los Angeles, as did Jim Conlee at KHTZ Los Angeles. Frank Shiers was my best friend at KRWM Seattle and still is. Turns out he was NOT my worst nightmare, LOL ☺ Ross 'Boss' Block rescued me from KAFF Radio in Flagstaff. Sam Bass at KyXy San Diego inspired me to paint word pictures on the air. KFOX's Russ Schell made it possible to return to SoCal and work in Redondo Beach with a great staff including Jim, Sharon, Doug, Kevin and Nick. Charlie Tuna inspired me beyond words with his amazing work in the K-HITS studio. Wolfman Jack was a genuinely nice man and a personal hero of mine. Gratitude to Joni Caryl for putting up with my Broncos bits on KLSX in L.A. KOST 103.5's Liz Kiley, Ted Ziegenbusch and Mike Sakellarides were so patient, and Mike has always been there for us. Jhani Kaye brought out the best in me.

Teri Griffin put up with me for 6 years at Coast 97.3 and Love 94 in SoFla and all she got out of it was a platter of fried shrimp and hot sauce. Nando laughed at all my jokes. Gustavo wasn't much of a talker, but he could communicate!

Paul Worrell at The Ridge in Blue Ridge rescued me from myself. Worship leader Mark Hartman has been more than kind. Worship leader Frank Fortner, Phil and Martha Boswell and the Church of Joy showed great respect for me even though I don't deserve it. Mike Cox, Billy Smith, Scott Custer, Joel Trice, David and Cindy Spangler and Christ Chapel provided an opportunity to learn. San Clemente Church of Christ 'forced' me to sing, LOL. Brian Simon at Pike County Church of Christ could talk to me without being preachy. Brian is a sincere, uber talented young minister. Thanks to Todd, John, Jena, Alex and Pike County Church of Christ.

Where would I be without 'The Hood'– Stones, Clites, Welchlens and Bradshaws for all of their love and support? (Miss you guys!) And to my prayer warriors in Pike and Fannin Counties here in Georgia as well as neighbors Jerry, Allen, Billy, Niky and Daniel, Jackie, David, Scott and Nancy. Nancy was one of the ICU nurses who attended to Kay in 2020.

Thank you, Jason Lee, Bill in the booth, and Bear Valley Community Church worship team, for believing in me. (And I loved it when you called me 'The Edge') Lakewood's Travis and Emily Branham deserve an attaboy and attagirl! Hugs and deep thanks to Reg and Amy Cox, Richard and Melanie Crane, Steve and Dawn Curtis for their support. Lots of hugs to the Lakewood Church of Christ for all their encouragement. JT and Stacy Cole have had undying support for me and my music. And Stacy's vocals rocked my music. Bobby Blume's music massaged my heart. Cary Gillaspie inspired my vision. Thank you! Eddy and Verla Ketchersid and Main Street Church of Christ and the West Seattle Church of Christ for your kindness.

Sincere thanks to the dozens more who helped me, inspired me and tolerated me along the way, including Jan and Kathy Blackwell, Gary and Terry Davenport, Bill and Sandy Lockhart, the West Broward Church of Christ, Bruce and Donna Mohr, Rick and Kathleen Hackman, Martin and Debbie Lira, and Diana and Ronnie Williams. Steve and Debbie Rew opened their home countless times to Kay and me . Thanks to Betty and Arnie Klemm, Mark and Debbie Talvitie and my high school friends who have always been there for me including Cindy Robinson Cochran, David Eckenrode, and Steve Bauer. Special love to the Dave Aregood Life Group who have been unbelievably supportive AND it was this Life Group who introduced me to Venmo (YAY!).

Sincere appreciation to Nicole Donoho, Logan Mungo and Xulon Press staff for their major assistance and patience. Nicole lived "rent free in my head for two months." (Thanks to Rush for that line ☺)

I have the deepest gratitude for the inspiration, support and love you all gave me to write *Culture Jock*.

+++

AIRCHECKS AND INTERVIEWS

INTERVIEWS

Leslie Nielsen	https://www.culturejock.net/
Gloria Estefan	https://www.culturejock.net/
Robert Duvall	https://www.culturejock.net/
Dave Barry	https://www.culturejock.net/

AIR CHECKS

San Antonio	1974	KTFM	https://www.culturejock.net/
Seattle	1993	KRWM	https://www.culturejock.net/
Chicago	1977	WLUP	https://www.culturejock.net/
Houston	1976	KLOL	https://www.culturejock.net/
Denver	2003	KJCD	https://www.culturejock.net/
Los Angeles	1982	KHTZ	https://www.culturejock.net/
China	1987	KyXy	https://www.culturejock.net/

TIMELINE

Places and Dates

Tampa	1947	BORN
Richmond	1950	MOVED FOR DAD'S COLLEGE
Houston	1954	DAD'S 1ST JOB, SHELL CHEM
Houston	1963-65	STEPHEN F. AUSTIN H.S.
San Antonio	1965	LACKLAND AFB
Colorado Springs	1965	USAFA PREP SCHOOL
Houston	1967	HONORABLY RESIGNED USAFA
Houston	1971	KAY GRADUATES DOBIE H.S.
Houston	1971	MARRIED TO KAY
Bryan-College Station	1973	KTAM/KORA
San Antonio	1974	KTFM
Houston	1976	KTFM to KLOL
Chicago	1977	KLOL to WLUP
Santa Monica	1978	WLUP to KZLA
Seattle	1979	KZLA to KZOK
Westchester	1980	KZOK to KFOX
Westchester	1981	KFOX to K-WEST

San Clemente	1981	K-WEST to KHTZ
San Clemente	1985	KHTZ to KFI/KOST
San Clemente	1986	KFI to KLSX
San Clemente	1987	SEPARATION and KyXy
San Clemente	1990	KJQY
San Clemente	1991	UNEMPLOYED/Freelance Videos
Flagstaff	1993	KAFF
Seattle	1993	KAFF to KRWM
Irvine	1995	KRWM to KACD
Seattle	1996	KJR-FM, KRWM
Coral Springs	1997	WFLC, Sam's near drowning
Plantation	2000	WLVE
Lakewood	2003	KJCD
Lakewood	2008	UNEMPLOYED/Freelance Audio
Lakewood	2010	K-LOVE, Air1 Radio Networks
Concord	2018	RETIREMENT
Lakewood	2016	RETIREMENT
Blue Ridge	2020	KAY DIAGNOSED WITH CANCER
Blue Ridge	2020	KAY's ER Event and Cardiac arrest
Blue Ridge	2021	50th Wedding Anniversary

REVIEWS

REVIEW by F. Lagard Smith, Author, *(The Daily Bible)*

Kenny Noble Cortes' breezy style, wicked sense of humor, insider look at the radio industry and deejay lifestyle, dashes of insight into interesting--sometimes famous people--makes *Culture Jock* a true "page turner." The spiritual thread that is almost teasingly woven throughout, keeps one on the edge of their seat, wondering just how bad a sinner this ignoble Noble really is!

Most important of all is the underlying, inescapable message which forces the reader to reflect on their own spiritual schizophrenia, discouraging bouts with temptation, and even one's own marital challenges.

There is just the right bit of preaching without crossing the line to being preachy. Just the right amount of confession and raw honesty without TMI, allowing the reader to relate, to be warned, to be rebuked, to be encouraged, to try harder, to be more Jesus dependent and grateful for God's loving, accepting grace. All of that happens in a short book that catches you off-guard.

+++

Smith has written some 30 books—legal, social, doctrinal, and devotional. He is most widely known as the compiler and narrator of "The Daily Bible," the NIV and NLT in chronological order.

REVIEW by Dave Logan, Radio Programmer

Kenny Noble Cortes shares his ups and downs openly and shows how his faith "saved him" time and time again. Living in that truth engages the reader as he tells his mesmerizing tale.

Culture Jock never comes across as preachy or holier-than-thou. There are times when KNC seems a little hard on himself, but only we know how we feel when we're tempted or, even worse, sensing we've failed our family as a husband, father, and provider. Those feelings could be stereotypical reactions, but also something many readers may relate to.

From a broadcasting perspective, we need to understand that our gift for sharing our lives with others behind the mic often touches people in a manner we don't fully appreciate or immediately understand. Culture Jock (One Foot in The World, One Foot in The Church) is that and more... a story of dreams broken and fulfilled.

+++

Veteran programmer Dave Logan has experience at the top levels of broadcasting, having programmed WNEW-FM/New York, WCBS-FM/New York, WLUP-FM/Chicago, KFOG-FM/San Francisco, and KBSG-FM/Seattle as well as helping launch XM Satellite Radio.

REVIEW by Frank Shiers, Seattle news anchor, writer, producer

"Pay no attention to that man behind the curtain."

In *Culture Jock*, author Kenny Noble Cortes brazenly ignores that admonition from the great and powerful Wizard of Oz. And in so doing, the longtime broadcaster gives us a rare peek backstage into the human and spiritual sides of the radio business.

Kenny speaks to readers in the same way he spoke with his countless radio listeners - intimately, openly, honestly, with a touch of humor. He's vulnerable, telling stories that resonate with those who hear them.

His struggles to live a truly Christian life, connect with our own. His stumbles are our stumbles. His successes give us hope. This book will, at times, make you sad, and at others, make you smile. It will also inspire you. That's all the more reason to pay attention to this man behind the curtain.

+++

Frank Shiers spent 35 years as a disc jockey, talk show host, and newsperson in Seattle. He worked at high profile stations like KLSY, KRWM, KBSG and KIRO. Shiers also worked with the author as co-host of the morning show at KRWM in the early to mid-90s.

REVIEW by Martin Crowe, former addict

Culture Jock is inspiring. Kenny Noble Cortes' transparency is brave and bold. This book will bless a million people's lives. As a man who struggled with addiction my whole life, I applaud him for dealing with it in a very brave manner. I believe many people have one foot in the world and one foot in the church. This book is a roadmap to inspire people to believe they can plant both feet in the presence of the Lord.

+++

Marty is a Medicare specialist and retirement analyst. He and his wife Laurie are close friends with the author and his family.

REVIEW by Paul Worrell, Elder, The Ridge, Blue Ridge, Georgia

There is no doubt that the Holy Spirit flowed out through Kenny Noble Cortes in this writing. That alone is a huge blessing for the reader. And I believe there is no doubt that God will use this book to touch many different people in many ways!

Sometimes the chronology takes a sharp turn, but Kenny's timeline continues to engage the reader even when you're not sure of the year or era. The reality is, Culture Jock creates a healthy interest and a sense of suspense.

The bottom line? I really liked Culture Jock and am looking forward to Kenny's adventures in 'Culture Jock 2' (One Foot on Earth, One Foot in Heaven)

www.ingramcontent.com/pod-product-compliance
Lightning Source LLC
LaVergne TN
LVHW091530070526
838199LV00001B/3